GStreamer Application Development Manual 1.8.3

A catalogue record for this book is available from the Hong Kong Public Libraries.

Published in Hong Kong by Samurai Media Limited.

Email: info@samuraimedia.org

ISBN 978-988-8406-65-4

Table of Contents

List of Figures

Foreword

GStreamer is an extremely powerful and versatile framework for creating streaming media applications. Many of the virtues of the GStreamer framework come from its modularity: GStreamer can seamlessly incorporate new plugin modules. But because modularity and power often come at a cost of greater complexity, writing new applications is not always easy.

This guide is intended to help you understand the GStreamer framework (version 1.8.3) so you can develop applications based on it. The first chapters will focus on development of a simple audio player, with much effort going into helping you understand GStreamer concepts. Later chapters will go into more advanced topics related to media playback, but also at other forms of media processing (capture, editing, etc.).

Introduction

1. Who should read this manual?

This book is about GStreamer from an application developer's point of view; it describes how to write a GStreamer application using the GStreamer libraries and tools. For an explanation about writing plugins, we suggest the Plugin Writers Guide (http://gstreamer.freedesktop.org/data/doc/gstreamer/head/pwg/html/index.html).

Also check out the other documentation available on the GStreamer web site (http://gstreamer.freedesktop.org/documentation/).

2. Preliminary reading

In order to understand this manual, you need to have a basic understanding of the *C language*.

Since GStreamer adheres to the GObject programming model, this guide also assumes that you understand the basics of GObject (http://library.gnome.org/devel/gobject/stable/) and glib (http://library.gnome.org/devel/glib/stable/) programming. Especially,

- GObject instantiation
- GObject properties (set/get)
- GObject casting
- GObject referecing/dereferencing
- glib memory management
- glib signals and callbacks
- glib main loop

3. Structure of this manual

To help you navigate through this guide, it is divided into several large parts. Each part addresses a particular broad topic concerning GStreamer appliction development. The parts of this guide are laid out in the following order:

Part I in *GStreamer Application Development Manual (1.8.3)* gives you an overview of GStreamer, it's design principles and foundations.

Part II in *GStreamer Application Development Manual (1.8.3)* covers the basics of GStreamer application programming. At the end of this part, you should be able to build your own audio player using GStreamer

In Part III in *GStreamer Application Development Manual (1.8.3)*, we will move on to advanced subjects which make GStreamer stand out of its competitors. We will discuss application-pipeline interaction using dynamic parameters and interfaces, we will discuss threading and threaded pipelines, scheduling and clocks (and synchronization). Most of those topics are not just there to introduce you to their API, but primarily to give a deeper insight in solving application programming problems with GStreamer and understanding their concepts.

Next, in Part IV in *GStreamer Application Development Manual (1.8.3)*, we will go into higher-level programming APIs for GStreamer. You don't exactly need to know all the details from the previous parts to understand this, but you will need to understand basic GStreamer concepts nevertheless. We will, amongst others, discuss XML, playbin and autopluggers.

Finally in Part V in *GStreamer Application Development Manual (1.8.3)*, you will find some random information on integrating with GNOME, KDE, OS X or Windows, some debugging help and general tips to improve and simplify GStreamer programming.

I. About GStreamer

This part gives you an overview of the technologies described in this book.

Chapter 1. What is GStreamer?

GStreamer is a framework for creating streaming media applications. The fundamental design comes from the video pipeline at Oregon Graduate Institute, as well as some ideas from DirectShow.

GStreamer's development framework makes it possible to write any type of streaming multimedia application. The GStreamer framework is designed to make it easy to write applications that handle audio or video or both. It isn't restricted to audio and video, and can process any kind of data flow. The pipeline design is made to have little overhead above what the applied filters induce. This makes GStreamer a good framework for designing even high-end audio applications which put high demands on latency.

One of the most obvious uses of GStreamer is using it to build a media player. GStreamer already includes components for building a media player that can support a very wide variety of formats, including MP3, Ogg/Vorbis, MPEG-1/2, AVI, Quicktime, mod, and more. GStreamer, however, is much more than just another media player. Its main advantages are that the pluggable components can be mixed and matched into arbitrary pipelines so that it's possible to write a full-fledged video or audio editing application.

The framework is based on plugins that will provide the various codec and other functionality. The plugins can be linked and arranged in a pipeline. This pipeline defines the flow of the data. Pipelines can also be edited with a GUI editor and saved as XML so that pipeline libraries can be made with a minimum of effort.

The GStreamer core function is to provide a framework for plugins, data flow and media type handling/negotiation. It also provides an API to write applications using the various plugins.

Specifically, GStreamer provides

- an API for multimedia applications
- a plugin architecture
- a pipeline architecture
- a mechanism for media type handling/negotiation
- a mechanism for synchronization
- over 250 plug-ins providing more than 1000 elements
- a set of tools

GStreamer plug-ins could be classified into

- protocols handling
- sources: for audio and video (involves protocol plugins)

- formats: parsers, formaters, muxers, demuxers, metadata, subtitles

- codecs: coders and decoders

- filters: converters, mixers, effects, ...

- sinks: for audio and video (involves protocol plugins)

Figure 1-1. Gstreamer overview

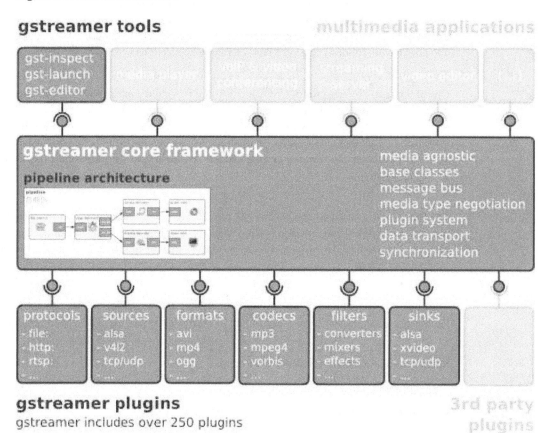

GStreamer is packaged into

- gstreamer: the core package

- gst-plugins-base: an essential exemplary set of elements

- gst-plugins-good: a set of good-quality plug-ins under LGPL

- gst-plugins-ugly: a set of good-quality plug-ins that might pose distribution problems

- gst-plugins-bad: a set of plug-ins that need more quality

- gst-libav: a set of plug-ins that wrap libav for decoding and encoding

- a few others packages

Chapter 2. Design principles

2.1. Clean and powerful

GStreamer provides a clean interface to:

- The application programmer who wants to build a media pipeline. The programmer can use an extensive set of powerful tools to create media pipelines without writing a single line of code. Performing complex media manipulations becomes very easy.

- The plugin programmer. Plugin programmers are provided a clean and simple API to create self-contained plugins. An extensive debugging and tracing mechanism has been integrated. GStreamer also comes with an extensive set of real-life plugins that serve as examples too.

2.2. Object oriented

GStreamer adheres to GObject, the GLib 2.0 object model. A programmer familiar with GLib 2.0 or GTK+ will be comfortable with GStreamer.

GStreamer uses the mechanism of signals and object properties.

All objects can be queried at runtime for their various properties and capabilities.

GStreamer intends to be similar in programming methodology to GTK+. This applies to the object model, ownership of objects, reference counting, etc.

2.3. Extensible

All GStreamer Objects can be extended using the GObject inheritance methods.

All plugins are loaded dynamically and can be extended and upgraded independently.

2.4. Allow binary-only plugins

Plugins are shared libraries that are loaded at runtime. Since all the properties of the plugin can be set using the GObject properties, there is no need (and in fact no way) to have any header files installed for the plugins.

Special care has been taken to make plugins completely self-contained. All relevant aspects of plugins can be queried at run-time.

2.5. High performance

High performance is obtained by:

- using GLib's `GSlice` allocator
- extremely light-weight links between plugins. Data can travel the pipeline with minimal overhead. Data passing between plugins only involves a pointer dereference in a typical pipeline.
- providing a mechanism to directly work on the target memory. A plugin can for example directly write to the X server's shared memory space. Buffers can also point to arbitrary memory, such as a sound card's internal hardware buffer.
- refcounting and copy on write minimize usage of memcpy. Sub-buffers efficiently split buffers into manageable pieces.
- dedicated streaming threads, with scheduling handled by the kernel.
- allowing hardware acceleration by using specialized plugins.
- using a plugin registry with the specifications of the plugins so that the plugin loading can be delayed until the plugin is actually used.

2.6. Clean core/plugins separation

The core of GStreamer is essentially media-agnostic. It only knows about bytes and blocks, and only contains basic elements. The core of GStreamer is functional enough to even implement low-level system tools, like cp.

All of the media handling functionality is provided by plugins external to the core. These tell the core how to handle specific types of media.

2.7. Provide a framework for codec experimentation

GStreamer also wants to be an easy framework where codec developers can experiment with different algorithms, speeding up the development of open and free multimedia codecs like those developed by the Xiph.Org Foundation (http://www.xiph.org) (such as Theora and Vorbis).

Chapter 3. Foundations

This chapter of the guide introduces the basic concepts of GStreamer. Understanding these concepts will be important in reading any of the rest of this guide, all of them assume understanding of these basic concepts.

3.1. Elements

An *element* is the most important class of objects in GStreamer. You will usually create a chain of elements linked together and let data flow through this chain of elements. An element has one specific function, which can be the reading of data from a file, decoding of this data or outputting this data to your sound card (or anything else). By chaining together several such elements, you create a *pipeline* that can do a specific task, for example media playback or capture. GStreamer ships with a large collection of elements by default, making the development of a large variety of media applications possible. If needed, you can also write new elements. That topic is explained in great deal in the *GStreamer Plugin Writer's Guide*.

3.2. Pads

Pads are element's input and output, where you can connect other elements. They are used to negotiate links and data flow between elements in GStreamer. A pad can be viewed as a "plug" or "port" on an element where links may be made with other elements, and through which data can flow to or from those elements. Pads have specific data handling capabilities: a pad can restrict the type of data that flows through it. Links are only allowed between two pads when the allowed data types of the two pads are compatible. Data types are negotiated between pads using a process called *caps negotiation*. Data types are described as a `GstCaps`.

An analogy may be helpful here. A pad is similar to a plug or jack on a physical device. Consider, for example, a home theater system consisting of an amplifier, a DVD player, and a (silent) video projector. Linking the DVD player to the amplifier is allowed because both devices have audio jacks, and linking the projector to the DVD player is allowed because both devices have compatible video jacks. Links between the projector and the amplifier may not be made because the projector and amplifier have different types of jacks. Pads in GStreamer serve the same purpose as the jacks in the home theater system.

For the most part, all data in GStreamer flows one way through a link between elements. Data flows out of one element through one or more *source pads*, and elements accept incoming data through one or more *sink pads*. Source and sink elements have only source and sink pads, respectively. Data usually means buffers (described by the `GstBuffer` (http://gstreamer.freedesktop.org/data/doc/gstreamer/stable/gstreamer/html/gstreamer-GstBuffer.html) object) and events (described by the `GstEvent` (http://gstreamer.freedesktop.org/data/doc/gstreamer/stable/gstreamer/html/gstreamer-GstEvent.html) object).

3.3. Bins and pipelines

A *bin* is a container for a collection of elements. Since bins are subclasses of elements themselves, you can mostly control a bin as if it were an element, thereby abstracting away a lot of complexity for your application. You can, for example change state on all elements in a bin by changing the state of that bin itself. Bins also forward bus messages from their contained children (such as error messages, tag messages or EOS messages).

A *pipeline* is a top-level bin. It provides a bus for the application and manages the synchronization for its children. As you set it to PAUSED or PLAYING state, data flow will start and media processing will take place. Once started, pipelines will run in a separate thread until you stop them or the end of the data stream is reached.

Figure 3-1. GStreamer pipeline for a simple ogg player

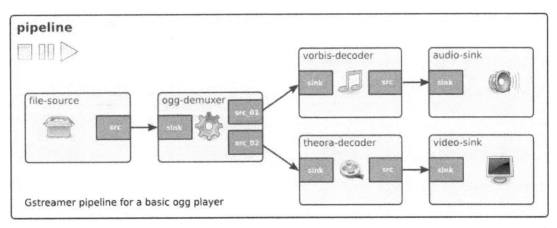

3.4. Communication

GStreamer provides several mechanisms for communication and data exchange between the *application* and the *pipeline*.

- *buffers* are objects for passing streaming data between elements in the pipeline. Buffers always travel from sources to sinks (downstream).
- *events* are objects sent between elements or from the application to elements. Events can travel upstream and downstream. Downstream events can be synchronised to the data flow.

- *messages* are objects posted by elements on the pipeline's message bus, where they will be held for collection by the application. Messages can be intercepted synchronously from the streaming thread context of the element posting the message, but are usually handled asynchronously by the application from the application's main thread. Messages are used to transmit information such as errors, tags, state changes, buffering state, redirects etc. from elements to the application in a thread-safe way.

- *queries* allow applications to request information such as duration or current playback position from the pipeline. Queries are always answered synchronously. Elements can also use queries to request information from their peer elements (such as the file size or duration). They can be used both ways within a pipeline, but upstream queries are more common.

Figure 3-2. GStreamer pipeline with different communication flows

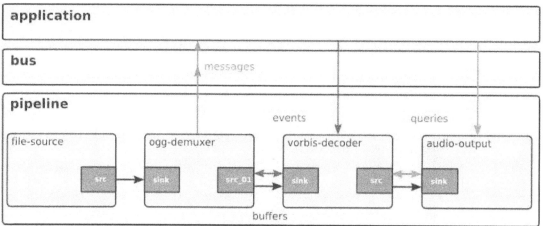

II. Building an Application

In these chapters, we will discuss the basic concepts of GStreamer and the most-used objects, such as elements, pads and buffers. We will use a visual representation of these objects so that we can visualize the more complex pipelines you will learn to build later on. You will get a first glance at the GStreamer API, which should be enough for building elementary applications. Later on in this part, you will also learn to build a basic command-line application.

Note that this part will give a look into the low-level API and concepts of GStreamer. Once you're going to build applications, you might want to use higher-level APIs. Those will be discussed later on in this manual.

Chapter 4. Initializing GStreamer

When writing a GStreamer application, you can simply include gst/gst.h to get access to the library functions. Besides that, you will also need to initialize the GStreamer library.

4.1. Simple initialization

Before the GStreamer libraries can be used, gst_init has to be called from the main application. This call will perform the necessary initialization of the library as well as parse the GStreamer-specific command line options.

A typical program [1] would have code to initialize GStreamer that looks like this:

Example 4-1. Initializing GStreamer

```c
#include <stdio.h>
#include <gst/gst.h>

int
main (int   argc,
      char *argv[])
{
  const gchar *nano_str;
  guint major, minor, micro, nano;

  gst_init (&argc, &argv);

  gst_version (&major, &minor, &micro, &nano);

  if (nano == 1)
    nano_str = "(CVS)";
  else if (nano == 2)
    nano_str = "(Prerelease)";
  else
    nano_str = "";

  printf ("This program is linked against GStreamer %d.%d.%d %s\n",
          major, minor, micro, nano_str);

  return 0;
}
```

Use the GST_VERSION_MAJOR, GST_VERSION_MINOR and GST_VERSION_MICRO macros to get the GStreamer version you are building against, or use the function `gst_version` to get the version your application is linked against. GStreamer currently uses a scheme where versions with the same major and minor versions are API-/ and ABI-compatible.

It is also possible to call the `gst_init` function with two NULL arguments, in which case no command line options will be parsed by GStreamer.

4.2. The GOption interface

You can also use a GOption table to initialize your own parameters as shown in the next example:

Example 4-2. Initialisation using the GOption interface

```c
#include <gst/gst.h>

int
main (int    argc,
      char *argv[])
{
  gboolean silent = FALSE;
  gchar *savefile = NULL;
  GOptionContext *ctx;
  GError *err = NULL;
  GOptionEntry entries[] = {
    { "silent", 's', 0, G_OPTION_ARG_NONE, &silent,
      "do not output status information", NULL },
    { "output", 'o', 0, G_OPTION_ARG_STRING, &savefile,
      "save xml representation of pipeline to FILE and exit", "FILE" },
    { NULL }
  };

  ctx = g_option_context_new ("- Your application");
  g_option_context_add_main_entries (ctx, entries, NULL);
  g_option_context_add_group (ctx, gst_init_get_option_group ());
  if (!g_option_context_parse (ctx, &argc, &argv, &err)) {
    g_print ("Failed to initialize: %s\n", err->message);
    g_clear_error (&err);
    g_option_context_free (ctx);
    return 1;
  }
  g_option_context_free (ctx);

  printf ("Run me with --help to see the Application options appended.\n");

  return 0;
}
```

As shown in this fragment, you can use a GOption
(http://developer.gnome.org/glib/stable/glib-Commandline-option-parser.html) table to define your
application-specific command line options, and pass this table to the GLib initialization function along
with the option group returned from the function `gst_init_get_option_group`. Your application
options will be parsed in addition to the standard GStreamer options.

Notes

1. The code for this example is automatically extracted from the documentation and built under
   `tests/examples/manual` in the GStreamer tarball.

Chapter 5. Elements

The most important object in GStreamer for the application programmer is the `GstElement` (http://gstreamer.freedesktop.org/data/doc/gstreamer/stable/gstreamer/html/GstElement.html) object. An element is the basic building block for a media pipeline. All the different high-level components you will use are derived from `GstElement`. Every decoder, encoder, demuxer, video or audio output is in fact a `GstElement`

5.1. What are elements?

For the application programmer, elements are best visualized as black boxes. On the one end, you might put something in, the element does something with it and something else comes out at the other side. For a decoder element, for example, you'd put in encoded data, and the element would output decoded data. In the next chapter (see Pads and capabilities), you will learn more about data input and output in elements, and how you can set that up in your application.

5.1.1. Source elements

Source elements generate data for use by a pipeline, for example reading from disk or from a sound card. Figure 5-1 shows how we will visualise a source element. We always draw a source pad to the right of the element.

Figure 5-1. Visualisation of a source element

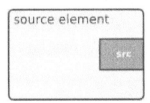

Source elements do not accept data, they only generate data. You can see this in the figure because it only has a source pad (on the right). A source pad can only generate data.

5.1.2. Filters, convertors, demuxers, muxers and codecs

Filters and filter-like elements have both input and outputs pads. They operate on data that they receive on their input (sink) pads, and will provide data on their output (source) pads. Examples of such elements are a volume element (filter), a video scaler (convertor), an Ogg demuxer or a Vorbis decoder.

Filter-like elements can have any number of source or sink pads. A video demuxer, for example, would have one sink pad and several (1-N) source pads, one for each elementary stream contained in the container format. Decoders, on the other hand, will only have one source and sink pads.

Figure 5-2. Visualisation of a filter element

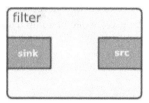

Figure 5-2 shows how we will visualise a filter-like element. This specific element has one source and one sink element. Sink pads, receiving input data, are depicted at the left of the element; source pads are still on the right.

Figure 5-3. Visualisation of a filter element with more than one output pad

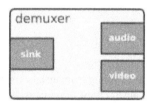

Figure 5-3 shows another filter-like element, this one having more than one output (source) pad. An example of one such element could, for example, be an Ogg demuxer for an Ogg stream containing both audio and video. One source pad will contain the elementary video stream, another will contain the elementary audio stream. Demuxers will generally fire signals when a new pad is created. The application programmer can then handle the new elementary stream in the signal handler.

5.1.3. Sink elements

Sink elements are end points in a media pipeline. They accept data but do not produce anything. Disk writing, soundcard playback, and video output would all be implemented by sink elements. Figure 5-4 shows a sink element.

Figure 5-4. Visualisation of a sink element

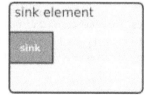

5.2. Creating a `GstElement`

The simplest way to create an element is to use `gst_element_factory_make ()`
(http://gstreamer.freedesktop.org/data/doc/gstreamer/stable/gstreamer/html/GstElementFactory.html#gst-element-factory-make). This function takes a factory name and an element name for the newly created element. The name of the element is something you can use later on to look up the element in a bin, for example. The name will also be used in debug output. You can pass NULL as the name argument to get a unique, default name.

When you don't need the element anymore, you need to unref it using `gst_object_unref ()`
(http://gstreamer.freedesktop.org/data/doc/gstreamer/stable/gstreamer/html/GstObject.html#gst-object-unref). This decreases the reference count for the element by 1. An element has a refcount of 1 when it gets created. An element gets destroyed completely when the refcount is decreased to 0.

The following example [1] shows how to create an element named *source* from the element factory named *fakesrc*. It checks if the creation succeeded. After checking, it unrefs the element.

```
#include <gst/gst.h>

int
main (int    argc,
      char *argv[])
{
  GstElement *element;

  /* init GStreamer */
  gst_init (&argc, &argv);

  /* create element */
  element = gst_element_factory_make ("fakesrc", "source");
  if (!element) {
    g_print ("Failed to create element of type 'fakesrc'\n");
    return -1;
  }

  gst_object_unref (GST_OBJECT (element));

  return 0;
}
```

`gst_element_factory_make` is actually a shorthand for a combination of two functions. A GstElement
(http://gstreamer.freedesktop.org/data/doc/gstreamer/stable/gstreamer/html/GstElement.html) object is created from a factory. To create the element, you have to get access to a GstElementFactory
(http://gstreamer.freedesktop.org/data/doc/gstreamer/stable/gstreamer/html/GstElementFactory.html) object using a unique factory name. This is done with `gst_element_factory_find ()`

(http://gstreamer.freedesktop.org/data/doc/gstreamer/stable/gstreamer/html/GstElementFactory.html#gst-element-factory-find).

The following code fragment is used to get a factory that can be used to create the *fakesrc* element, a fake data source. The function `gst_element_factory_create ()` (http://gstreamer.freedesktop.org/data/doc/gstreamer/stable/gstreamer/html/GstElementFactory.html#gst-element-factory-create) will use the element factory to create an element with the given name.

```
#include <gst/gst.h>

int
main (int   argc,
      char *argv[])
{
  GstElementFactory *factory;
  GstElement * element;

  /* init GStreamer */
  gst_init (&argc, &argv);

  /* create element, method #2 */
  factory = gst_element_factory_find ("fakesrc");
  if (!factory) {
    g_print ("Failed to find factory of type 'fakesrc'\n");
    return -1;
  }
  element = gst_element_factory_create (factory, "source");
  if (!element) {
    g_print ("Failed to create element, even though its factory exists!\n");
    return -1;
  }

  gst_object_unref (GST_OBJECT (element));

  return 0;
}
```

5.3. Using an element as a `GObject`

A `GstElement` (http://gstreamer.freedesktop.org/data/doc/gstreamer/stable/gstreamer/html/GstElement.html) can have several properties which are implemented using standard `GObject` properties. The usual `GObject` methods to query, set and get property values and `GParamSpecs` are therefore supported.

Every GstElement inherits at least one property from its parent GstObject: the "name" property. This is the name you provide to the functions gst_element_factory_make () or gst_element_factory_create (). You can get and set this property using the functions gst_object_set_name and gst_object_get_name or use the GObject property mechanism as shown below.

```
#include <gst/gst.h>

int
main (int    argc,
      char *argv[])
{
  GstElement *element;
  gchar *name;

  /* init GStreamer */
  gst_init (&argc, &argv);

  /* create element */
  element = gst_element_factory_make ("fakesrc", "source");

  /* get name */
  g_object_get (G_OBJECT (element), "name", &name, NULL);
  g_print ("The name of the element is '%s'.\n", name);
  g_free (name);

  gst_object_unref (GST_OBJECT (element));

  return 0;
}
```

Most plugins provide additional properties to provide more information about their configuration or to configure the element. **gst-inspect** is a useful tool to query the properties of a particular element, it will also use property introspection to give a short explanation about the function of the property and about the parameter types and ranges it supports. See Section 23.4.2 in the appendix for details about **gst-inspect**.

For more information about GObject properties we recommend you read the GObject manual (http://developer.gnome.org/gobject/stable/rn01.html) and an introduction to The Glib Object system (http://developer.gnome.org/gobject/stable/pt01.html).

A GstElement (http://gstreamer.freedesktop.org/data/doc/gstreamer/stable/gstreamer/html/GstElement.html) also provides various GObject signals that can be used as a flexible callback mechanism. Here, too, you can use **gst-inspect** to see which signals a specific element supports. Together, signals and properties are the most basic way in which elements and applications interact.

5.4. More about element factories

In the previous section, we briefly introduced the `GstElementFactory`
(http://gstreamer.freedesktop.org/data/doc/gstreamer/stable/gstreamer/html/GstElementFactory.html)
object already as a way to create instances of an element. Element factories, however, are much more
than just that. Element factories are the basic types retrieved from the GStreamer registry, they describe
all plugins and elements that GStreamer can create. This means that element factories are useful for
automated element instancing, such as what autopluggers do, and for creating lists of available elements.

5.4.1. Getting information about an element using a factory

Tools like **gst-inspect** will provide some generic information about an element, such as the person that
wrote the plugin, a descriptive name (and a shortname), a rank and a category. The category can be used
to get the type of the element that can be created using this element factory. Examples of categories
include `Codec/Decoder/Video` (video decoder), `Codec/Encoder/Video` (video encoder),
`Source/Video` (a video generator), `Sink/Video` (a video output), and all these exist for audio as well,
of course. Then, there's also `Codec/Demuxer` and `Codec/Muxer` and a whole lot more. **gst-inspect** will
give a list of all factories, and **gst-inspect <factory-name>** will list all of the above information, and a
lot more.

```
#include <gst/gst.h>

int
main (int    argc,
      char *argv[])
{
  GstElementFactory *factory;

  /* init GStreamer */
  gst_init (&argc, &argv);

  /* get factory */
  factory = gst_element_factory_find ("fakesrc");
  if (!factory) {
    g_print ("You don't have the 'fakesrc' element installed!\n");
    return -1;
  }

  /* display information */
  g_print ("The '%s' element is a member of the category %s.\n"
           "Description: %s\n",
           gst_plugin_feature_get_name (GST_PLUGIN_FEATURE (factory)),
           gst_element_factory_get_metadata (factory, GST_ELEMENT_METADATA_KLASS),
           gst_element_factory_get_metadata (factory, GST_ELEMENT_METADATA_DESCRIPTION))

  return 0;
}
```

You can use `gst_registry_pool_feature_list` `(GST_TYPE_ELEMENT_FACTORY)` to get a list of all the element factories that GStreamer knows about.

5.4.2. Finding out what pads an element can contain

Perhaps the most powerful feature of element factories is that they contain a full description of the pads that the element can generate, and the capabilities of those pads (in layman words: what types of media can stream over those pads), without actually having to load those plugins into memory. This can be used to provide a codec selection list for encoders, or it can be used for autoplugging purposes for media players. All current GStreamer-based media players and autopluggers work this way. We'll look closer at these features as we learn about `GstPad` and `GstCaps` in the next chapter: Pads and capabilities

5.5. Linking elements

By linking a source element with zero or more filter-like elements and finally a sink element, you set up a media pipeline. Data will flow through the elements. This is the basic concept of media handling in GStreamer.

Figure 5-5. Visualisation of three linked elements

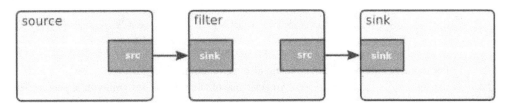

By linking these three elements, we have created a very simple chain of elements. The effect of this will be that the output of the source element ("element1") will be used as input for the filter-like element ("element2"). The filter-like element will do something with the data and send the result to the final sink element ("element3").

Imagine the above graph as a simple Ogg/Vorbis audio decoder. The source is a disk source which reads the file from disc. The second element is a Ogg/Vorbis audio decoder. The sink element is your soundcard, playing back the decoded audio data. We will use this simple graph to construct an Ogg/Vorbis player later in this manual.

In code, the above graph is written like this:

```
#include <gst/gst.h>

int
```

```
main (int    argc,
      char *argv[])
{
  GstElement *pipeline;
  GstElement *source, *filter, *sink;

  /* init */
  gst_init (&argc, &argv);

  /* create pipeline */
  pipeline = gst_pipeline_new ("my-pipeline");

  /* create elements */
  source = gst_element_factory_make ("fakesrc", "source");
  filter = gst_element_factory_make ("identity", "filter");
  sink = gst_element_factory_make ("fakesink", "sink");

  /* must add elements to pipeline before linking them */
  gst_bin_add_many (GST_BIN (pipeline), source, filter, sink, NULL);

  /* link */
  if (!gst_element_link_many (source, filter, sink, NULL)) {
    g_warning ("Failed to link elements!");
  }

[..]

}
```

For more specific behaviour, there are also the functions gst_element_link () and gst_element_link_pads (). You can also obtain references to individual pads and link those using various gst_pad_link_* () functions. See the API references for more details.

Important: you must add elements to a bin or pipeline *before* linking them, since adding an element to a bin will disconnect any already existing links. Also, you cannot directly link elements that are not in the same bin or pipeline; if you want to link elements or pads at different hierarchy levels, you will need to use ghost pads (more about ghost pads later, see Section 8.4).

5.6. Element States

After being created, an element will not actually perform any actions yet. You need to change elements state to make it do something. GStreamer knows four element states, each with a very specific meaning. Those four states are:

- GST_STATE_NULL: this is the default state. No resources are allocated in this state, so, transitioning to it will free all resources. The element must be in this state when its refcount reaches 0 and it is freed.

- `GST_STATE_READY`: in the ready state, an element has allocated all of its global resources, that is, resources that can be kept within streams. You can think about opening devices, allocating buffers and so on. However, the stream is not opened in this state, so the stream positions is automatically zero. If a stream was previously opened, it should be closed in this state, and position, properties and such should be reset.

- `GST_STATE_PAUSED`: in this state, an element has opened the stream, but is not actively processing it. An element is allowed to modify a stream's position, read and process data and such to prepare for playback as soon as state is changed to PLAYING, but it is *not* allowed to play the data which would make the clock run. In summary, PAUSED is the same as PLAYING but without a running clock.

  Elements going into the PAUSED state should prepare themselves for moving over to the PLAYING state as soon as possible. Video or audio outputs would, for example, wait for data to arrive and queue it so they can play it right after the state change. Also, video sinks can already play the first frame (since this does not affect the clock yet). Autopluggers could use this same state transition to already plug together a pipeline. Most other elements, such as codecs or filters, do not need to explicitly do anything in this state, however.

- `GST_STATE_PLAYING`: in the PLAYING state, an element does exactly the same as in the PAUSED state, except that the clock now runs.

You can change the state of an element using the function `gst_element_set_state ()`. If you set an element to another state, GStreamer will internally traverse all intermediate states. So if you set an element from NULL to PLAYING, GStreamer will internally set the element to READY and PAUSED in between.

When moved to `GST_STATE_PLAYING`, pipelines will process data automatically. They do not need to be iterated in any form. Internally, GStreamer will start threads that take this task on to them. GStreamer will also take care of switching messages from the pipeline's thread into the application's own thread, by using a `GstBus` (http://gstreamer.freedesktop.org/data/doc/gstreamer/stable/gstreamer/html/GstBus.html). See Chapter 7 for details.

When you set a bin or pipeline to a certain target state, it will usually propagate the state change to all elements within the bin or pipeline automatically, so it's usually only necessary to set the state of the top-level pipeline to start up the pipeline or shut it down. However, when adding elements dynamically to an already-running pipeline, e.g. from within a "pad-added" signal callback, you need to set it to the desired target state yourself using `gst_element_set_state ()` or `gst_element_sync_state_with_parent ()`.

Notes

1. The code for this example is automatically extracted from the documentation and built under `tests/examples/manual` in the GStreamer tarball.

Chapter 6. Bins

A bin is a container element. You can add elements to a bin. Since a bin is an element itself, a bin can be handled in the same way as any other element. Therefore, the whole previous chapter (Elements) applies to bins as well.

6.1. What are bins

Bins allow you to combine a group of linked elements into one logical element. You do not deal with the individual elements anymore but with just one element, the bin. We will see that this is extremely powerful when you are going to construct complex pipelines since it allows you to break up the pipeline in smaller chunks.

The bin will also manage the elements contained in it. It will perform state changes on the elements as well as collect and forward bus messages.

Figure 6-1. Visualisation of a bin with some elements in it

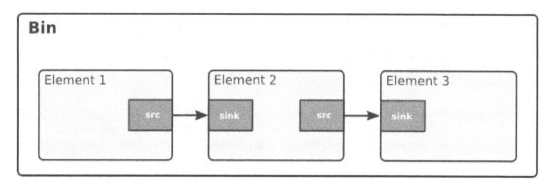

There is one specialized type of bin available to the GStreamer programmer:

- A pipeline: a generic container that manages the synchronization and bus messages of the contained elements. The toplevel bin has to be a pipeline, every application thus needs at least one of these.

6.2. Creating a bin

Bins are created in the same way that other elements are created, i.e. using an element factory. There are also convenience functions available (gst_bin_new () and gst_pipeline_new ()). To add elements to a bin or remove elements from a bin, you can use gst_bin_add () and gst_bin_remove (). Note that the bin that you add an element to will take ownership of that element. If you destroy the bin, the element will be dereferenced with it. If you remove an element from a bin, it will be dereferenced automatically.

```
#include <gst/gst.h>

int
main (int   argc,
      char *argv[])
{
  GstElement *bin, *pipeline, *source, *sink;

  /* init */
  gst_init (&argc, &argv);

  /* create */
  pipeline = gst_pipeline_new ("my_pipeline");
  bin = gst_bin_new ("my_bin");
  source = gst_element_factory_make ("fakesrc", "source");
  sink = gst_element_factory_make ("fakesink", "sink");

  /* First add the elements to the bin */
  gst_bin_add_many (GST_BIN (bin), source, sink, NULL);
  /* add the bin to the pipeline */
  gst_bin_add (GST_BIN (pipeline), bin);

  /* link the elements */
  gst_element_link (source, sink);

[..]

}
```

There are various functions to lookup elements in a bin. The most commonly used are `gst_bin_get_by_name ()` and `gst_bin_get_by_interface ()`. You can also iterate over all elements that a bin contains using the function `gst_bin_iterate_elements ()`. See the API references of `GstBin` (http://gstreamer.freedesktop.org/data/doc/gstreamer/stable/gstreamer/html/GstBin.html) for details.

6.3. Custom bins

The application programmer can create custom bins packed with elements to perform a specific task. This allows you, for example, to write an Ogg/Vorbis decoder with just the following lines of code:

```
int
main (int   argc,
      char *argv[])
{
  GstElement *player;
```

```
/* init */
gst_init (&argc, &argv);

/* create player */
player = gst_element_factory_make ("oggvorbisplayer", "player");

/* set the source audio file */
g_object_set (player, "location", "helloworld.ogg", NULL);

/* start playback */
gst_element_set_state (GST_ELEMENT (player), GST_STATE_PLAYING);
[..]
}
```

(This is a silly example of course, there already exists a much more powerful and versatile custom bin like this: the playbin element.)

Custom bins can be created with a plugin or from the application. You will find more information about creating custom bin in the Plugin Writers Guide (http://gstreamer.freedesktop.org/data/doc/gstreamer/head/pwg/html/index.html).

Examples of such custom bins are the playbin and uridecodebin elements from gst-plugins-base (http://gstreamer.freedesktop.org/data/doc/gstreamer/head/gst-plugins-base-plugins/html/index.html).

6.4. Bins manage states of their children

Bins manage the state of all elements contained in them. If you set a bin (or a pipeline, which is a special top-level type of bin) to a certain target state using `gst_element_set_state ()`, it will make sure all elements contained within it will also be set to this state. This means it's usually only necessary to set the state of the top-level pipeline to start up the pipeline or shut it down.

The bin will perform the state changes on all its children from the sink element to the source element. This ensures that the downstream element is ready to receive data when the upstream element is brought to PAUSED or PLAYING. Similarly when shutting down, the sink elements will be set to READY or NULL first, which will cause the upstream elements to receive a FLUSHING error and stop the streaming threads before the elements are set to the READY or NULL state.

Note, however, that if elements are added to a bin or pipeline that's already running, , e.g. from within a "pad-added" signal callback, its state will not automatically be brought in line with the current state or target state of the bin or pipeline it was added to. Instead, you have to need to set it to the desired target state yourself using `gst_element_set_state ()` or `gst_element_sync_state_with_parent ()` when adding elements to an already-running pipeline.

Chapter 7. Bus

A bus is a simple system that takes care of forwarding messages from the streaming threads to an application in its own thread context. The advantage of a bus is that an application does not need to be thread-aware in order to use GStreamer, even though GStreamer itself is heavily threaded.

Every pipeline contains a bus by default, so applications do not need to create a bus or anything. The only thing applications should do is set a message handler on a bus, which is similar to a signal handler to an object. When the mainloop is running, the bus will periodically be checked for new messages, and the callback will be called when any message is available.

7.1. How to use a bus

There are two different ways to use a bus:

- Run a GLib/Gtk+ main loop (or iterate the default GLib main context yourself regularly) and attach some kind of watch to the bus. This way the GLib main loop will check the bus for new messages and notify you whenever there are messages.

  Typically you would use `gst_bus_add_watch ()` or `gst_bus_add_signal_watch ()` in this case.

  To use a bus, attach a message handler to the bus of a pipeline using `gst_bus_add_watch ()`. This handler will be called whenever the pipeline emits a message to the bus. In this handler, check the signal type (see next section) and do something accordingly. The return value of the handler should be TRUE to keep the handler attached to the bus, return FALSE to remove it.

- Check for messages on the bus yourself. This can be done using `gst_bus_peek ()` and/or `gst_bus_poll ()`.

```
#include <gst/gst.h>

static GMainLoop *loop;

static gboolean
my_bus_callback (GstBus      *bus,
 GstMessage *message,
 gpointer    data)
{
  g_print ("Got %s message\n", GST_MESSAGE_TYPE_NAME (message));

  switch (GST_MESSAGE_TYPE (message)) {
```

```
        case GST_MESSAGE_ERROR: {
          GError *err;
          gchar *debug;

          gst_message_parse_error (message, &err, &debug);
          g_print ("Error: %s\n", err->message);
          g_error_free (err);
          g_free (debug);

          g_main_loop_quit (loop);
          break;
        }
        case GST_MESSAGE_EOS:
          /* end-of-stream */
          g_main_loop_quit (loop);
          break;
        default:
          /* unhandled message */
          break;
    }

    /* we want to be notified again the next time there is a message
     * on the bus, so returning TRUE (FALSE means we want to stop watching
     * for messages on the bus and our callback should not be called again)
     */
    return TRUE;
}

gint
main (gint   argc,
      gchar *argv[])
{
  GstElement *pipeline;
  GstBus *bus;
  guint bus_watch_id;

  /* init */
  gst_init (&argc, &argv);

  /* create pipeline, add handler */
  pipeline = gst_pipeline_new ("my_pipeline");

  /* adds a watch for new message on our pipeline's message bus to
   * the default GLib main context, which is the main context that our
   * GLib main loop is attached to below
   */
  bus = gst_pipeline_get_bus (GST_PIPELINE (pipeline));
  bus_watch_id = gst_bus_add_watch (bus, my_bus_callback, NULL);
  gst_object_unref (bus);

[..]

  /* create a mainloop that runs/iterates the default GLib main context
```

```
 * (context NULL), in other words: makes the context check if anything
 * it watches for has happened. When a message has been posted on the
 * bus, the default main context will automatically call our
 * my_bus_callback() function to notify us of that message.
 * The main loop will be run until someone calls g_main_loop_quit()
 */
loop = g_main_loop_new (NULL, FALSE);
g_main_loop_run (loop);

/* clean up */
gst_element_set_state (pipeline, GST_STATE_NULL);
gst_object_unref (pipeline);
g_source_remove (bus_watch_id);
g_main_loop_unref (loop);

return 0;
}
```

It is important to know that the handler will be called in the thread context of the mainloop. This means that the interaction between the pipeline and application over the bus is *asynchronous*, and thus not suited for some real-time purposes, such as cross-fading between audio tracks, doing (theoretically) gapless playback or video effects. All such things should be done in the pipeline context, which is easiest by writing a GStreamer plug-in. It is very useful for its primary purpose, though: passing messages from pipeline to application. The advantage of this approach is that all the threading that GStreamer does internally is hidden from the application and the application developer does not have to worry about thread issues at all.

Note that if you're using the default GLib mainloop integration, you can, instead of attaching a watch, connect to the "message" signal on the bus. This way you don't have to switch() on all possible message types; just connect to the interesting signals in form of "message::<type>", where <type> is a specific message type (see the next section for an explanation of message types).

The above snippet could then also be written as:

```
GstBus *bus;

[..]

bus = gst_pipeline_get_bus (GST_PIPELINE (pipeline);
gst_bus_add_signal_watch (bus);
g_signal_connect (bus, "message::error", G_CALLBACK (cb_message_error), NULL);
g_signal_connect (bus, "message::eos", G_CALLBACK (cb_message_eos), NULL);

[..]
```

If you aren't using GLib mainloop, the asynchronous message signals won't be available by default. You can however install a custom sync handler that wakes up the custom mainloop and that uses `gst_bus_async_signal_func ()` to emit the signals. (see also documentation (http://gstreamer.freedesktop.org/data/doc/gstreamer/stable/gstreamer/html/GstBus.html) for details)

7.2. Message types

GStreamer has a few pre-defined message types that can be passed over the bus. The messages are extensible, however. Plug-ins can define additional messages, and applications can decide to either have specific code for those or ignore them. All applications are strongly recommended to at least handle error messages by providing visual feedback to the user.

All messages have a message source, type and timestamp. The message source can be used to see which element emitted the message. For some messages, for example, only the ones emitted by the top-level pipeline will be interesting to most applications (e.g. for state-change notifications). Below is a list of all messages and a short explanation of what they do and how to parse message-specific content.

- Error, warning and information notifications: those are used by elements if a message should be shown to the user about the state of the pipeline. Error messages are fatal and terminate the data-passing. The error should be repaired to resume pipeline activity. Warnings are not fatal, but imply a problem nevertheless. Information messages are for non-problem notifications. All those messages contain a `GError` with the main error type and message, and optionally a debug string. Both can be extracted using `gst_message_parse_error ()`, `_parse_warning ()` and `_parse_info ()`. Both error and debug strings should be freed after use.

- End-of-stream notification: this is emitted when the stream has ended. The state of the pipeline will not change, but further media handling will stall. Applications can use this to skip to the next song in their playlist. After end-of-stream, it is also possible to seek back in the stream. Playback will then continue automatically. This message has no specific arguments.

- Tags: emitted when metadata was found in the stream. This can be emitted multiple times for a pipeline (e.g. once for descriptive metadata such as artist name or song title, and another one for stream-information, such as samplerate and bitrate). Applications should cache metadata internally. `gst_message_parse_tag ()` should be used to parse the taglist, which should be `gst_tag_list_unref ()`'ed when no longer needed.

- State-changes: emitted after a successful state change. `gst_message_parse_state_changed ()` can be used to parse the old and new state of this transition.

- Buffering: emitted during caching of network-streams. One can manually extract the progress (in percent) from the message by extracting the "buffer-percent" property from the structure returned by `gst_message_get_structure ()`. See also Chapter 15.

- Element messages: these are special messages that are unique to certain elements and usually represent additional features. The element's documentation should mention in detail which element messages a particular element may send. As an example, the 'qtdemux' QuickTime demuxer element may send a 'redirect' element message on certain occasions if the stream contains a redirect instruction.

- Application-specific messages: any information on those can be extracted by getting the message structure (see above) and reading its fields. Usually these messages can safely be ignored.

Application messages are primarily meant for internal use in applications in case the application needs to marshal information from some thread into the main thread. This is particularly useful when the application is making use of element signals (as those signals will be emitted in the context of the streaming thread).

Chapter 8. Pads and capabilities

As we have seen in Elements, the pads are the element's interface to the outside world. Data streams from one element's source pad to another element's sink pad. The specific type of media that the element can handle will be exposed by the pad's capabilities. We will talk more on capabilities later in this chapter (see Section 8.2).

8.1. Pads

A pad type is defined by two properties: its direction and its availability. As we've mentioned before, GStreamer defines two pad directions: source pads and sink pads. This terminology is defined from the view of within the element: elements receive data on their sink pads and generate data on their source pads. Schematically, sink pads are drawn on the left side of an element, whereas source pads are drawn on the right side of an element. In such graphs, data flows from left to right. [1]

Pad directions are very simple compared to pad availability. A pad can have any of three availabilities: always, sometimes and on request. The meaning of those three types is exactly as it says: always pads always exist, sometimes pad exist only in certain cases (and can disappear randomly), and on-request pads appear only if explicitly requested by applications.

8.1.1. Dynamic (or sometimes) pads

Some elements might not have all of their pads when the element is created. This can happen, for example, with an Ogg demuxer element. The element will read the Ogg stream and create dynamic pads for each contained elementary stream (vorbis, theora) when it detects such a stream in the Ogg stream. Likewise, it will delete the pad when the stream ends. This principle is very useful for demuxer elements, for example.

Running gst-inspect oggdemux will show that the element has only one pad: a sink pad called 'sink'. The other pads are "dormant". You can see this in the pad template because there is an "Exists: Sometimes" property. Depending on the type of Ogg file you play, the pads will be created. We will see that this is very important when you are going to create dynamic pipelines. You can attach a signal handler to an element to inform you when the element has created a new pad from one of its "sometimes" pad templates. The following piece of code is an example of how to do this:

```
#include <gst/gst.h>

static void
cb_new_pad (GstElement *element,
    GstPad      *pad,
    gpointer    data)
{
  gchar *name;
```

```
  name = gst_pad_get_name (pad);
  g_print ("A new pad %s was created\n", name);
  g_free (name);

  /* here, you would setup a new pad link for the newly created pad */
[..]

}

int
main (int    argc,
      char *argv[])
{
  GstElement *pipeline, *source, *demux;
  GMainLoop *loop;

  /* init */
  gst_init (&argc, &argv);

  /* create elements */
  pipeline = gst_pipeline_new ("my_pipeline");
  source = gst_element_factory_make ("filesrc", "source");
  g_object_set (source, "location", argv[1], NULL);
  demux = gst_element_factory_make ("oggdemux", "demuxer");

  /* you would normally check that the elements were created properly */

  /* put together a pipeline */
  gst_bin_add_many (GST_BIN (pipeline), source, demux, NULL);
  gst_element_link_pads (source, "src", demux, "sink");

  /* listen for newly created pads */
  g_signal_connect (demux, "pad-added", G_CALLBACK (cb_new_pad), NULL);

  /* start the pipeline */
  gst_element_set_state (GST_ELEMENT (pipeline), GST_STATE_PLAYING);
  loop = g_main_loop_new (NULL, FALSE);
  g_main_loop_run (loop);

[..]

}
```

It is not uncommon to add elements to the pipeline only from within the "pad-added" callback. If you do this, don't forget to set the state of the newly-added elements to the target state of the pipeline using `gst_element_set_state ()` or `gst_element_sync_state_with_parent ()`.

8.1.2. Request pads

An element can also have request pads. These pads are not created automatically but are only created on demand. This is very useful for multiplexers, aggregators and tee elements. Aggregators are elements that merge the content of several input streams together into one output stream. Tee elements are the reverse: they are elements that have one input stream and copy this stream to each of their output pads, which are created on request. Whenever an application needs another copy of the stream, it can simply request a new output pad from the tee element.

The following piece of code shows how you can request a new output pad from a "tee" element:

```
static void
some_function (GstElement *tee)
{
  GstPad * pad;
  gchar *name;

  pad = gst_element_get_request_pad (tee, "src%d");
  name = gst_pad_get_name (pad);
  g_print ("A new pad %s was created\n", name);
  g_free (name);

  /* here, you would link the pad */
[..]

  /* and, after doing that, free our reference */
  gst_object_unref (GST_OBJECT (pad));
}
```

The `gst_element_get_request_pad ()` method can be used to get a pad from the element based on the name of the pad template. It is also possible to request a pad that is compatible with another pad template. This is very useful if you want to link an element to a multiplexer element and you need to request a pad that is compatible. The method `gst_element_get_compatible_pad ()` can be used to request a compatible pad, as shown in the next example. It will request a compatible pad from an Ogg multiplexer from any input.

```
static void
link_to_multiplexer (GstPad      *tolink_pad,
     GstElement *mux)
{
  GstPad *pad;
  gchar *srcname, *sinkname;

  srcname = gst_pad_get_name (tolink_pad);
  pad = gst_element_get_compatible_pad (mux, tolink_pad);
  gst_pad_link (tolinkpad, pad);
  sinkname = gst_pad_get_name (pad);
  gst_object_unref (GST_OBJECT (pad));
```

```
    g_print ("A new pad %s was created and linked to %s\n", sinkname, srcname);
    g_free (sinkname);
    g_free (srcname);
}
```

8.2. Capabilities of a pad

Since the pads play a very important role in how the element is viewed by the outside world, a mechanism is implemented to describe the data that can flow or currently flows through the pad by using capabilities. Here, we will briefly describe what capabilities are and how to use them, enough to get an understanding of the concept. For an in-depth look into capabilities and a list of all capabilities defined in GStreamer, see the Plugin Writers Guide (http://gstreamer.freedesktop.org/data/doc/gstreamer/head/pwg/html/index.html).

Capabilities are attached to pad templates and to pads. For pad templates, it will describe the types of media that may stream over a pad created from this template. For pads, it can either be a list of possible caps (usually a copy of the pad template's capabilities), in which case the pad is not yet negotiated, or it is the type of media that currently streams over this pad, in which case the pad has been negotiated already.

8.2.1. Dissecting capabilities

A pad's capabilities are described in a `GstCaps` object. Internally, a `GstCaps` (http://gstreamer.freedesktop.org/data/doc/gstreamer/stable/gstreamer/html/gstreamer-GstCaps.html) will contain one or more `GstStructure` (http://gstreamer.freedesktop.org/data/doc/gstreamer/stable/gstreamer/html/gstreamer-GstStructure.html) that will describe one media type. A negotiated pad will have capabilities set that contain exactly *one* structure. Also, this structure will contain only *fixed* values. These constraints are not true for unnegotiated pads or pad templates.

As an example, below is a dump of the capabilities of the "vorbisdec" element, which you will get by running **gst-inspect vorbisdec**. You will see two pads: a source and a sink pad. Both of these pads are always available, and both have capabilities attached to them. The sink pad will accept vorbis-encoded audio data, with the media type "audio/x-vorbis". The source pad will be used to send raw (decoded) audio samples to the next element, with a raw audio media type (in this case, "audio/x-raw"). The source pad will also contain properties for the audio samplerate and the amount of channels, plus some more that you don't need to worry about for now.

```
Pad Templates:
  SRC template: 'src'
    Availability: Always
    Capabilities:
```

```
audio/x-raw
          format: F32LE
            rate: [ 1, 2147483647 ]
        channels: [ 1, 256 ]

SINK template: 'sink'
  Availability: Always
  Capabilities:
    audio/x-vorbis
```

8.2.2. Properties and values

Properties are used to describe extra information for capabilities. A property consists of a key (a string) and a value. There are different possible value types that can be used:

- Basic types, this can be pretty much any `GType` registered with Glib. Those properties indicate a specific, non-dynamic value for this property. Examples include:

  - An integer value (`G_TYPE_INT`): the property has this exact value.

  - A boolean value (`G_TYPE_BOOLEAN`): the property is either TRUE or FALSE.

  - A float value (`G_TYPE_FLOAT`): the property has this exact floating point value.

  - A string value (`G_TYPE_STRING`): the property contains a UTF-8 string.

  - A fraction value (`GST_TYPE_FRACTION`): contains a fraction expressed by an integer numerator and denominator.

- Range types are `GTypes` registered by GStreamer to indicate a range of possible values. They are used for indicating allowed audio samplerate values or supported video sizes. The two types defined in GStreamer are:

  - An integer range value (`GST_TYPE_INT_RANGE`): the property denotes a range of possible integers, with a lower and an upper boundary. The "vorbisdec" element, for example, has a rate property that can be between 8000 and 50000.

  - A float range value (`GST_TYPE_FLOAT_RANGE`): the property denotes a range of possible floating point values, with a lower and an upper boundary.

  - A fraction range value (`GST_TYPE_FRACTION_RANGE`): the property denotes a range of possible fraction values, with a lower and an upper boundary.

- A list value (`GST_TYPE_LIST`): the property can take any value from a list of basic values given in this list.

  Example: caps that express that either a sample rate of 44100 Hz and a sample rate of 48000 Hz is supported would use a list of integer values, with one value being 44100 and one value being 48000.

- An array value (GST_TYPE_ARRAY): the property is an array of values. Each value in the array is a full value on its own, too. All values in the array should be of the same elementary type. This means that an array can contain any combination of integers, lists of integers, integer ranges together, and the same for floats or strings, but it can not contain both floats and ints at the same time.

Example: for audio where there are more than two channels involved the channel layout needs to be specified (for one and two channel audio the channel layout is implicit unless stated otherwise in the caps). So the channel layout would be an array of integer enum values where each enum value represents a loudspeaker position. Unlike a GST_TYPE_LIST, the values in an array will be interpreted as a whole.

8.3. What capabilities are used for

Capabilities (short: caps) describe the type of data that is streamed between two pads, or that one pad (template) supports. This makes them very useful for various purposes:

- Autoplugging: automatically finding elements to link to a pad based on its capabilities. All autopluggers use this method.

- Compatibility detection: when two pads are linked, GStreamer can verify if the two pads are talking about the same media type. The process of linking two pads and checking if they are compatible is called "caps negotiation".

- Metadata: by reading the capabilities from a pad, applications can provide information about the type of media that is being streamed over the pad, which is information about the stream that is currently being played back.

- Filtering: an application can use capabilities to limit the possible media types that can stream between two pads to a specific subset of their supported stream types. An application can, for example, use "filtered caps" to set a specific (fixed or non-fixed) video size that should stream between two pads. You will see an example of filtered caps later in this manual, in Section 19.2. You can do caps filtering by inserting a capsfilter element into your pipeline and setting its "caps" property. Caps filters are often placed after converter elements like audioconvert, audioresample, videoconvert or videoscale to force those converters to convert data to a specific output format at a certain point in a stream.

8.3.1. Using capabilities for metadata

A pad can have a set (i.e. one or more) of capabilities attached to it. Capabilities (GstCaps) are represented as an array of one or more GstStructures, and each GstStructure is an array of fields where each field consists of a field name string (e.g. "width") and a typed value (e.g. G_TYPE_INT or GST_TYPE_INT_RANGE).

Note that there is a distinct difference between the *possible* capabilities of a pad (ie. usually what you find as caps of pad templates as they are shown in gst-inspect), the *allowed* caps of a pad (can be the same as the pad's template caps or a subset of them, depending on the possible caps of the peer pad) and lastly *negotiated* caps (these describe the exact format of a stream or buffer and contain exactly one structure and have no variable bits like ranges or lists, ie. they are fixed caps).

You can get values of properties in a set of capabilities by querying individual properties of one structure. You can get a structure from a caps using `gst_caps_get_structure ()` and the number of structures in a `GstCaps` using `gst_caps_get_size ()`.

Caps are called *simple caps* when they contain only one structure, and *fixed caps* when they contain only one structure and have no variable field types (like ranges or lists of possible values). Two other special types of caps are *ANY caps* and *empty caps*.

Here is an example of how to extract the width and height from a set of fixed video caps:

```
static void
read_video_props (GstCaps *caps)
{
  gint width, height;
  const GstStructure *str;

  g_return_if_fail (gst_caps_is_fixed (caps));

  str = gst_caps_get_structure (caps, 0);
  if (!gst_structure_get_int (str, "width", &width) ||
      !gst_structure_get_int (str, "height", &height)) {
    g_print ("No width/height available\n");
    return;
  }

  g_print ("The video size of this set of capabilities is %dx%d\n",
   width, height);
}
```

8.3.2. Creating capabilities for filtering

While capabilities are mainly used inside a plugin to describe the media type of the pads, the application programmer often also has to have basic understanding of capabilities in order to interface with the plugins, especially when using filtered caps. When you're using filtered caps or fixation, you're limiting the allowed types of media that can stream between two pads to a subset of their supported media types. You do this using a `capsfilter` element in your pipeline. In order to do this, you also need to create your own `GstCaps`. The easiest way to do this is by using the convenience function `gst_caps_new_simple ()`:

```
static gboolean
link_elements_with_filter (GstElement *element1, GstElement *element2)
{
  gboolean link_ok;
  GstCaps *caps;

  caps = gst_caps_new_simple ("video/x-raw",
        "format", G_TYPE_STRING, "I420",
      "width", G_TYPE_INT, 384,
      "height", G_TYPE_INT, 288,
      "framerate", GST_TYPE_FRACTION, 25, 1,
      NULL);

  link_ok = gst_element_link_filtered (element1, element2, caps);
  gst_caps_unref (caps);

  if (!link_ok) {
    g_warning ("Failed to link element1 and element2!");
  }

  return link_ok;
}
```

This will force the data flow between those two elements to a certain video format, width, height and framerate (or the linking will fail if that cannot be achieved in the context of the elements involved). Keep in mind that when you use `gst_element_link_filtered ()` it will automatically create a `capsfilter` element for you and insert it into your bin or pipeline between the two elements you want to connect (this is important if you ever want to disconnect those elements because then you will have to disconnect both elements from the capsfilter instead).

In some cases, you will want to create a more elaborate set of capabilities to filter a link between two pads. Then, this function is too simplistic and you'll want to use the method `gst_caps_new_full ()`:

```
static gboolean
link_elements_with_filter (GstElement *element1, GstElement *element2)
{
  gboolean link_ok;
  GstCaps *caps;

  caps = gst_caps_new_full (
      gst_structure_new ("video/x-raw",
 "width", G_TYPE_INT, 384,
 "height", G_TYPE_INT, 288,
 "framerate", GST_TYPE_FRACTION, 25, 1,
 NULL),
      gst_structure_new ("video/x-bayer",
 "width", G_TYPE_INT, 384,
 "height", G_TYPE_INT, 288,
 "framerate", GST_TYPE_FRACTION, 25, 1,
 NULL),
      NULL);
```

```
link_ok = gst_element_link_filtered (element1, element2, caps);
gst_caps_unref (caps);

if (!link_ok) {
  g_warning ("Failed to link element1 and element2!");
}

return link_ok;
}
```

See the API references for the full API of `GstStructure`
(http://gstreamer.freedesktop.org/data/doc/gstreamer/stable/gstreamer/html/gstreamer-GstStructure.html)
and `GstCaps`
(http://gstreamer.freedesktop.org/data/doc/gstreamer/stable/gstreamer/html/gstreamer-GstCaps.html).

8.4. Ghost pads

You can see from Figure 8-1 how a bin has no pads of its own. This is where "ghost pads" come into play.

**Figure 8-1. Visualisation of a `GstBin`
(http://gstreamer.freedesktop.org/data/doc/gstreamer/stable/gstreamer/html/GstBin.html) element
without ghost pads**

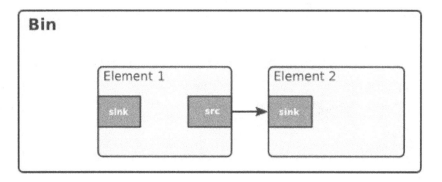

A ghost pad is a pad from some element in the bin that can be accessed directly from the bin as well.
Compare it to a symbolic link in UNIX filesystems. Using ghost pads on bins, the bin also has a pad and
can transparently be used as an element in other parts of your code.

**Figure 8-2. Visualisation of a `GstBin`
(http://gstreamer.freedesktop.org/data/doc/gstreamer/stable/gstreamer/html/GstBin.html) element
with a ghost pad**

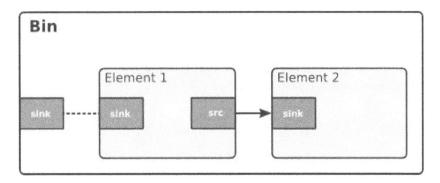

Figure 8-2 is a representation of a ghost pad. The sink pad of element one is now also a pad of the bin.
Because ghost pads look and work like any other pads, they can be added to any type of elements, not
just to a `GstBin`, just like ordinary pads.

A ghostpad is created using the function `gst_ghost_pad_new ()`:

```
#include <gst/gst.h>

int
main (int   argc,
      char *argv[])
{
  GstElement *bin, *sink;
  GstPad *pad;

  /* init */
  gst_init (&argc, &argv);

  /* create element, add to bin */
  sink = gst_element_factory_make ("fakesink", "sink");
  bin = gst_bin_new ("mybin");
  gst_bin_add (GST_BIN (bin), sink);

  /* add ghostpad */
  pad = gst_element_get_static_pad (sink, "sink");
  gst_element_add_pad (bin, gst_ghost_pad_new ("sink", pad));
  gst_object_unref (GST_OBJECT (pad));

[..]

}
```

In the above example, the bin now also has a pad: the pad called "sink" of the given element. The bin can, from here on, be used as a substitute for the sink element. You could, for example, link another element to the bin.

Notes

1. In reality, there is no objection to data flowing from a source pad to the sink pad of an element upstream (to the left of this element in drawings). Data will, however, always flow from a source pad of one element to the sink pad of another.

Chapter 9. Buffers and Events

The data flowing through a pipeline consists of a combination of buffers and events. Buffers contain the actual media data. Events contain control information, such as seeking information and end-of-stream notifiers. All this will flow through the pipeline automatically when it's running. This chapter is mostly meant to explain the concept to you; you don't need to do anything for this.

9.1. Buffers

Buffers contain the data that will flow through the pipeline you have created. A source element will typically create a new buffer and pass it through a pad to the next element in the chain. When using the GStreamer infrastructure to create a media pipeline you will not have to deal with buffers yourself; the elements will do that for you.

A buffer consists, amongst others, of:

- Pointers to memory objects. Memory objects encapsulate a region in the memory.
- A timestamp for the buffer.
- A refcount that indicates how many elements are using this buffer. This refcount will be used to destroy the buffer when no element has a reference to it.
- Buffer flags.

The simple case is that a buffer is created, memory allocated, data put in it, and passed to the next element. That element reads the data, does something (like creating a new buffer and decoding into it), and unreferences the buffer. This causes the data to be free'ed and the buffer to be destroyed. A typical video or audio decoder works like this.

There are more complex scenarios, though. Elements can modify buffers in-place, i.e. without allocating a new one. Elements can also write to hardware memory (such as from video-capture sources) or memory allocated from the X-server (using XShm). Buffers can be read-only, and so on.

9.2. Events

Events are control particles that are sent both up- and downstream in a pipeline along with buffers. Downstream events notify fellow elements of stream states. Possible events include seeking, flushes, end-of-stream notifications and so on. Upstream events are used both in application-element interaction as well as element-element interaction to request changes in stream state, such as seeks. For applications, only upstream events are important. Downstream events are just explained to get a more complete picture of the data concept.

Since most applications seek in time units, our example below does so too:

```
static void
seek_to_time (GstElement *element,
      guint64     time_ns)
{
  GstEvent *event;

  event = gst_event_new_seek (1.0, GST_FORMAT_TIME,
      GST_SEEK_FLAG_NONE,
      GST_SEEK_METHOD_SET, time_ns,
      GST_SEEK_TYPE_NONE, G_GUINT64_CONSTANT (0));
  gst_element_send_event (element, event);
}
```

The function `gst_element_seek ()` is a shortcut for this. This is mostly just to show how it all works.

Chapter 10. Your first application

This chapter will summarize everything you've learned in the previous chapters. It describes all aspects of a simple GStreamer application, including initializing libraries, creating elements, packing elements together in a pipeline and playing this pipeline. By doing all this, you will be able to build a simple Ogg/Vorbis audio player.

10.1. Hello world

We're going to create a simple first application, a simple Ogg/Vorbis command-line audio player. For this, we will use only standard GStreamer components. The player will read a file specified on the command-line. Let's get started!

We've learned, in Chapter 4, that the first thing to do in your application is to initialize GStreamer by calling gst_init (). Also, make sure that the application includes gst/gst.h so all function names and objects are properly defined. Use #include <gst/gst.h> to do that.

Next, you'll want to create the different elements using gst_element_factory_make (). For an Ogg/Vorbis audio player, we'll need a source element that reads files from a disk. GStreamer includes this element under the name "filesrc". Next, we'll need something to parse the file and decode it into raw audio. GStreamer has two elements for this: the first parses Ogg streams into elementary streams (video, audio) and is called "oggdemux". The second is a Vorbis audio decoder, it's conveniently called "vorbisdec". Since "oggdemux" creates dynamic pads for each elementary stream, you'll need to set a "pad-added" event handler on the "oggdemux" element, like you've learned in Section 8.1.1, to link the Ogg demuxer and the Vorbis decoder elements together. At last, we'll also need an audio output element, we will use "autoaudiosink", which automatically detects your audio device.

The last thing left to do is to add all elements into a container element, a GstPipeline, and wait until we've played the whole song. We've previously learned how to add elements to a container bin in Chapter 6, and we've learned about element states in Section 5.6. We will also attach a message handler to the pipeline bus so we can retrieve errors and detect the end-of-stream.

Let's now add all the code together to get our very first audio player:

```
#include <gst/gst.h>
#include <glib.h>


static gboolean
bus_call (GstBus      *bus,
          GstMessage *msg,
          gpointer    data)
```

```
{
  GMainLoop *loop = (GMainLoop *) data;

  switch (GST_MESSAGE_TYPE (msg)) {

    case GST_MESSAGE_EOS:
      g_print ("End of stream\n");
      g_main_loop_quit (loop);
      break;

    case GST_MESSAGE_ERROR: {
      gchar  *debug;
      GError *error;

      gst_message_parse_error (msg, &error, &debug);
      g_free (debug);

      g_printerr ("Error: %s\n", error->message);
      g_error_free (error);

      g_main_loop_quit (loop);
      break;
    }
    default:
      break;
  }

  return TRUE;
}


static void
on_pad_added (GstElement *element,
              GstPad     *pad,
              gpointer    data)
{
  GstPad *sinkpad;
  GstElement *decoder = (GstElement *) data;

  /* We can now link this pad with the vorbis-decoder sink pad */
  g_print ("Dynamic pad created, linking demuxer/decoder\n");

  sinkpad = gst_element_get_static_pad (decoder, "sink");

  gst_pad_link (pad, sinkpad);

  gst_object_unref (sinkpad);
}



int
main (int    argc,
```

```
        char *argv[])
{
  GMainLoop *loop;

  GstElement *pipeline, *source, *demuxer, *decoder, *conv, *sink;
  GstBus *bus;
  guint bus_watch_id;

  /* Initialisation */
  gst_init (&argc, &argv);

  loop = g_main_loop_new (NULL, FALSE);


  /* Check input arguments */
  if (argc != 2) {
    g_printerr ("Usage: %s <Ogg/Vorbis filename>\n", argv[0]);
    return -1;
  }


  /* Create gstreamer elements */
  pipeline = gst_pipeline_new ("audio-player");
  source   = gst_element_factory_make ("filesrc",      "file-source");
  demuxer  = gst_element_factory_make ("oggdemux",     "ogg-demuxer");
  decoder  = gst_element_factory_make ("vorbisdec",    "vorbis-decoder");
  conv     = gst_element_factory_make ("audioconvert", "converter");
  sink     = gst_element_factory_make ("autoaudiosink", "audio-output");

  if (!pipeline || !source || !demuxer || !decoder || !conv || !sink) {
    g_printerr ("One element could not be created. Exiting.\n");
    return -1;
  }

  /* Set up the pipeline */

  /* we set the input filename to the source element */
  g_object_set (G_OBJECT (source), "location", argv[1], NULL);

  /* we add a message handler */
  bus = gst_pipeline_get_bus (GST_PIPELINE (pipeline));
  bus_watch_id = gst_bus_add_watch (bus, bus_call, loop);
  gst_object_unref (bus);

  /* we add all elements into the pipeline */
  /* file-source | ogg-demuxer | vorbis-decoder | converter | alsa-output */
  gst_bin_add_many (GST_BIN (pipeline),
                    source, demuxer, decoder, conv, sink, NULL);

  /* we link the elements together */
  /* file-source -> ogg-demuxer ~> vorbis-decoder -> converter -> alsa-output */
  gst_element_link (source, demuxer);
  gst_element_link_many (decoder, conv, sink, NULL);
```

```
g_signal_connect (demuxer, "pad-added", G_CALLBACK (on_pad_added), decoder);

/* note that the demuxer will be linked to the decoder dynamically.
   The reason is that Ogg may contain various streams (for example
   audio and video). The source pad(s) will be created at run time,
   by the demuxer when it detects the amount and nature of streams.
   Therefore we connect a callback function which will be executed
   when the "pad-added" is emitted.*/


/* Set the pipeline to "playing" state*/
g_print ("Now playing: %s\n", argv[1]);
gst_element_set_state (pipeline, GST_STATE_PLAYING);


/* Iterate */
g_print ("Running...\n");
g_main_loop_run (loop);


/* Out of the main loop, clean up nicely */
g_print ("Returned, stopping playback\n");
gst_element_set_state (pipeline, GST_STATE_NULL);

g_print ("Deleting pipeline\n");
gst_object_unref (GST_OBJECT (pipeline));
g_source_remove (bus_watch_id);
g_main_loop_unref (loop);

return 0;
}
```

We now have created a complete pipeline. We can visualise the pipeline as follows:

Figure 10-1. The "hello world" pipeline

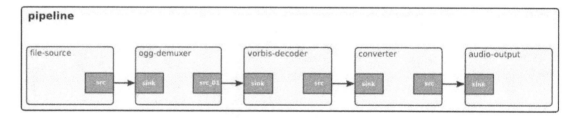

10.2. Compiling and Running helloworld.c

To compile the helloworld example, use: **gcc -Wall helloworld.c -o helloworld $(pkg-config --cflags --libs gstreamer-1.0)**. GStreamer makes use of **pkg-config** to get compiler and linker flags needed to compile this application.

If you're running a non-standard installation (ie. you've installed GStreamer from source yourself instead of using pre-built packages), make sure the `PKG_CONFIG_PATH` environment variable is set to the correct location (`$libdir/pkgconfig`).

In the unlikely case that you are using an uninstalled GStreamer setup (ie. gst-uninstalled), you will need to use libtool to build the hello world program, like this: **libtool --mode=link gcc -Wall helloworld.c -o helloworld $(pkg-config --cflags --libs gstreamer-1.0)**.

You can run this example application with **./helloworld file.ogg**. Substitute `file.ogg` with your favourite Ogg/Vorbis file.

10.3. Conclusion

This concludes our first example. As you see, setting up a pipeline is very low-level but powerful. You will see later in this manual how you can create a more powerful media player with even less effort using higher-level interfaces. We will discuss all that in
Part IV in *GStreamer Application Development Manual (1.8.3)*. We will first, however, go more in-depth into more advanced GStreamer internals.

It should be clear from the example that we can very easily replace the "filesrc" element with some other element that reads data from a network, or some other data source element that is better integrated with your desktop environment. Also, you can use other decoders and parsers/demuxers to support other media types. You can use another audio sink if you're not running Linux, but Mac OS X, Windows or FreeBSD, or you can instead use a filesink to write audio files to disk instead of playing them back. By using an audio card source, you can even do audio capture instead of playback. All this shows the reusability of GStreamer elements, which is its greatest advantage.

III. Advanced GStreamer concepts

In this part we will cover the more advanced features of GStreamer. With the basics you learned in the previous part you should be able to create a *simple* application. However, GStreamer provides much more candy than just the basics of playing back audio files. In this chapter, you will learn more of the low-level features and internals of GStreamer.

Some parts of this part will serve mostly as an explanation of how GStreamer works internally; they are not actually needed for actual application development. This includes chapters such as the ones covering scheduling, autoplugging and synchronization. Other chapters, however, discuss more advanced ways of pipeline-application interaction, and can turn out to be very useful for certain applications. This includes the chapters on metadata, querying and events, interfaces, dynamic parameters and pipeline data manipulation.

Chapter 11. Position tracking and seeking

So far, we've looked at how to create a pipeline to do media processing and how to make it run. Most application developers will be interested in providing feedback to the user on media progress. Media players, for example, will want to show a slider showing the progress in the song, and usually also a label indicating stream length. Transcoding applications will want to show a progress bar on how much percent of the task is done. GStreamer has built-in support for doing all this using a concept known as *querying*. Since seeking is very similar, it will be discussed here as well. Seeking is done using the concept of *events*.

11.1. Querying: getting the position or length of a stream

Querying is defined as requesting a specific stream property related to progress tracking. This includes getting the length of a stream (if available) or getting the current position. Those stream properties can be retrieved in various formats such as time, audio samples, video frames or bytes. The function most commonly used for this is gst_element_query (), although some convenience wrappers are provided as well (such as gst_element_query_position () and gst_element_query_duration ()). You can generally query the pipeline directly, and it'll figure out the internal details for you, like which element to query.

Internally, queries will be sent to the sinks, and "dispatched" backwards until one element can handle it; that result will be sent back to the function caller. Usually, that is the demuxer, although with live sources (from a webcam), it is the source itself.

```
#include <gst/gst.h>



static gboolean
cb_print_position (GstElement *pipeline)
{
  gint64 pos, len;

  if (gst_element_query_position (pipeline, GST_FORMAT_TIME, &pos)
    && gst_element_query_duration (pipeline, GST_FORMAT_TIME, &len)) {
    g_print ("Time: %" GST_TIME_FORMAT " / %" GST_TIME_FORMAT "\r",
     GST_TIME_ARGS (pos), GST_TIME_ARGS (len));
  }

  /* call me again */
  return TRUE;
}

gint
```

```
main (gint    argc,
      gchar *argv[])
{
  GstElement *pipeline;

[..]

  /* run pipeline */
  g_timeout_add (200, (GSourceFunc) cb_print_position, pipeline);
  g_main_loop_run (loop);

[..]

}
```

11.2. Events: seeking (and more)

Events work in a very similar way as queries. Dispatching, for example, works exactly the same for events (and also has the same limitations), and they can similarly be sent to the toplevel pipeline and it will figure out everything for you. Although there are more ways in which applications and elements can interact using events, we will only focus on seeking here. This is done using the seek-event. A seek-event contains a playback rate, a seek offset format (which is the unit of the offsets to follow, e.g. time, audio samples, video frames or bytes), optionally a set of seeking-related flags (e.g. whether internal buffers should be flushed), a seek method (which indicates relative to what the offset was given), and seek offsets. The first offset (cur) is the new position to seek to, while the second offset (stop) is optional and specifies a position where streaming is supposed to stop. Usually it is fine to just specify GST_SEEK_TYPE_NONE and -1 as end_method and end offset. The behaviour of a seek is also wrapped in the gst_element_seek ().

```
static void
seek_to_time (GstElement *pipeline,
      gint64      time_nanoseconds)
{
  if (!gst_element_seek (pipeline, 1.0, GST_FORMAT_TIME, GST_SEEK_FLAG_FLUSH,
                         GST_SEEK_TYPE_SET, time_nanoseconds,
                         GST_SEEK_TYPE_NONE, GST_CLOCK_TIME_NONE)) {
    g_print ("Seek failed!\n");
  }
}
```

Seeks with the GST_SEEK_FLAG_FLUSH should be done when the pipeline is in PAUSED or PLAYING state. The pipeline will automatically go to preroll state until the new data after the seek will cause the pipeline to preroll again. After the pipeline is prerolled, it will go back to the state (PAUSED or PLAYING) it was in when the seek was executed. You can wait (blocking) for the seek to complete with gst_element_get_state () or by waiting for the ASYNC_DONE message to appear on the bus.

Seeks without the GST_SEEK_FLAG_FLUSH should only be done when the pipeline is in the PLAYING state. Executing a non-flushing seek in the PAUSED state might deadlock because the pipeline streaming threads might be blocked in the sinks.

It is important to realise that seeks will not happen instantly in the sense that they are finished when the function gst_element_seek () returns. Depending on the specific elements involved, the actual seeking might be done later in another thread (the streaming thread), and it might take a short time until buffers from the new seek position will reach downstream elements such as sinks (if the seek was non-flushing then it might take a bit longer).

It is possible to do multiple seeks in short time-intervals, such as a direct response to slider movement. After a seek, internally, the pipeline will be paused (if it was playing), the position will be re-set internally, the demuxers and decoders will decode from the new position onwards and this will continue until all sinks have data again. If it was playing originally, it will be set to playing again, too. Since the new position is immediately available in a video output, you will see the new frame, even if your pipeline is not in the playing state.

Chapter 12. Metadata

GStreamer makes a clear distinction between two types of metadata, and has support for both types. The first is stream tags, which describe the content of a stream in a non-technical way. Examples include the author of a song, the title of that very same song or the album it is a part of. The other type of metadata is stream-info, which is a somewhat technical description of the properties of a stream. This can include video size, audio samplerate, codecs used and so on. Tags are handled using the GStreamer tagging system. Stream-info can be retrieved from a `GstPad` by getting the current (negotiated) `GstCaps` for that pad.

12.1. Metadata reading

Stream information can most easily be read by reading it from a `GstPad`. This has already been discussed before in Section 8.3.1. Therefore, we will skip it here. Note that this requires access to all pads of which you want stream information.

Tag reading is done through a bus in GStreamer, which has been discussed previously in Chapter 7. You can listen for `GST_MESSAGE_TAG` messages and handle them as you wish.

Note, however, that the `GST_MESSAGE_TAG` message may be fired multiple times in the pipeline. It is the application's responsibility to put all those tags together and display them to the user in a nice, coherent way. Usually, using `gst_tag_list_merge ()` is a good enough way of doing this; make sure to empty the cache when loading a new song, or after every few minutes when listening to internet radio. Also, make sure you use `GST_TAG_MERGE_PREPEND` as merging mode, so that a new title (which came in later) has a preference over the old one for display.

The following example will extract tags from a file and print them:

```
/* compile with:
 * gcc -o tags tags.c `pkg-config --cflags --libs gstreamer-1.0` */
#include <gst/gst.h>

static void
print_one_tag (const GstTagList * list, const gchar * tag, gpointer user_data)
{
  int i, num;

  num = gst_tag_list_get_tag_size (list, tag);
  for (i = 0; i < num; ++i) {
    const GValue *val;

    /* Note: when looking for specific tags, use the gst_tag_list_get_xyz() API,
     * we only use the GValue approach here because it is more generic */
    val = gst_tag_list_get_value_index (list, tag, i);
    if (G_VALUE_HOLDS_STRING (val)) {
```

```
          g_print ("\t%20s : %s\n", tag, g_value_get_string (val));
        } else if (G_VALUE_HOLDS_UINT (val)) {
          g_print ("\t%20s : %u\n", tag, g_value_get_uint (val));
        } else if (G_VALUE_HOLDS_DOUBLE (val)) {
          g_print ("\t%20s : %g\n", tag, g_value_get_double (val));
        } else if (G_VALUE_HOLDS_BOOLEAN (val)) {
          g_print ("\t%20s : %s\n", tag,
              (g_value_get_boolean (val)) ? "true" : "false");
        } else if (GST_VALUE_HOLDS_BUFFER (val)) {
          GstBuffer *buf = gst_value_get_buffer (val);
          guint buffer_size = gst_buffer_get_size (buf);

          g_print ("\t%20s : buffer of size %u\n", tag, buffer_size);
        } else if (GST_VALUE_HOLDS_DATE_TIME (val)) {
          GstDateTime *dt = g_value_get_boxed (val);
          gchar *dt_str = gst_date_time_to_iso8601_string (dt);

          g_print ("\t%20s : %s\n", tag, dt_str);
          g_free (dt_str);
        } else {
          g_print ("\t%20s : tag of type '%s'\n", tag, G_VALUE_TYPE_NAME (val));
        }
    }
}

static void
on_new_pad (GstElement * dec, GstPad * pad, GstElement * fakesink)
{
  GstPad *sinkpad;

  sinkpad = gst_element_get_static_pad (fakesink, "sink");
  if (!gst_pad_is_linked (sinkpad)) {
    if (gst_pad_link (pad, sinkpad) != GST_PAD_LINK_OK)
      g_error ("Failed to link pads!");
  }
  gst_object_unref (sinkpad);
}

int
main (int argc, char ** argv)
{
  GstElement *pipe, *dec, *sink;
  GstMessage *msg;
  gchar *uri;

  gst_init (&argc, &argv);

  if (argc < 2)
    g_error ("Usage: %s FILE or URI", argv[0]);

  if (gst_uri_is_valid (argv[1])) {
    uri = g_strdup (argv[1]);
  } else {
```

```
    uri = gst_filename_to_uri (argv[1], NULL);
  }

  pipe = gst_pipeline_new ("pipeline");

  dec = gst_element_factory_make ("uridecodebin", NULL);
  g_object_set (dec, "uri", uri, NULL);
  gst_bin_add (GST_BIN (pipe), dec);

  sink = gst_element_factory_make ("fakesink", NULL);
  gst_bin_add (GST_BIN (pipe), sink);

  g_signal_connect (dec, "pad-added", G_CALLBACK (on_new_pad), sink);

  gst_element_set_state (pipe, GST_STATE_PAUSED);

  while (TRUE) {
    GstTagList *tags = NULL;

    msg = gst_bus_timed_pop_filtered (GST_ELEMENT_BUS (pipe),
        GST_CLOCK_TIME_NONE,
        GST_MESSAGE_ASYNC_DONE | GST_MESSAGE_TAG | GST_MESSAGE_ERROR);

    if (GST_MESSAGE_TYPE (msg) != GST_MESSAGE_TAG) /* error or async_done */
      break;

    gst_message_parse_tag (msg, &tags);

    g_print ("Got tags from element %s:\n", GST_OBJECT_NAME (msg->src));
    gst_tag_list_foreach (tags, print_one_tag, NULL);
    g_print ("\n");
    gst_tag_list_unref (tags);

    gst_message_unref (msg);
  }

  if (GST_MESSAGE_TYPE (msg) == GST_MESSAGE_ERROR) {
    GError *err = NULL;

    gst_message_parse_error (msg, &err, NULL);
    g_printerr ("Got error: %s\n", err->message);
    g_error_free (err);
  }

  gst_message_unref (msg);
  gst_element_set_state (pipe, GST_STATE_NULL);
  gst_object_unref (pipe);
  g_free (uri);
  return 0;
}
```

12.2. Tag writing

Tag writing is done using the `GstTagSetter`
(http://gstreamer.freedesktop.org/data/doc/gstreamer/stable/gstreamer/html/GstTagSetter.html) interface.
All that's required is a tag-set-supporting element in your pipeline. In order to see if any of the elements
in your pipeline supports tag writing, you can use the function
`gst_bin_iterate_all_by_interface (pipeline, GST_TYPE_TAG_SETTER)`. On the resulting
element, usually an encoder or muxer, you can use `gst_tag_setter_merge ()` (with a taglist) or
`gst_tag_setter_add ()` (with individual tags) to set tags on it.

A nice extra feature in GStreamer tag support is that tags are preserved in pipelines. This means that if
you transcode one file containing tags into another media type, and that new media type supports tags
too, then the tags will be handled as part of the data stream and be merged into the newly written media
file, too.

Chapter 13. Interfaces

In Section 5.3, you have learned how to use `GObject` properties as a simple way to do interaction between applications and elements. This method suffices for the simple'n'straight settings, but fails for anything more complicated than a getter and setter. For the more complicated use cases, GStreamer uses interfaces based on the GObject `GTypeInterface` (http://library.gnome.org/devel/gobject/stable/gtype-non-instantiable-classed.html) type.

Most of the interfaces handled here will not contain any example code. See the API references for details. Here, we will just describe the scope and purpose of each interface.

13.1. The URI interface

In all examples so far, we have only supported local files through the "filesrc" element. GStreamer, obviously, supports many more location sources. However, we don't want applications to need to know any particular element implementation details, such as element names for particular network source types and so on. Therefore, there is a URI interface, which can be used to get the source element that supports a particular URI type. There is no strict rule for URI naming, but in general we follow naming conventions that others use, too. For example, assuming you have the correct plugins installed, GStreamer supports "file:///<path>/<file>", "http://<host>/<path>/<file>", "mms://<host>/<path>/<file>", and so on.

In order to get the source or sink element supporting a particular URI, use `gst_element_make_from_uri ()`, with the URI type being either `GST_URI_SRC` for a source element, or `GST_URI_SINK` for a sink element.

You can convert filenames to and from URIs using GLib's `g_filename_to_uri ()` and `g_uri_to_filename ()`.

13.2. The Color Balance interface

The colorbalance interface is a way to control video-related properties on an element, such as brightness, contrast and so on. It's sole reason for existence is that, as far as its authors know, there's no way to dynamically register properties using `GObject`.

The colorbalance interface is implemented by several plugins, including xvimagesink and the Video4linux2 elements.

13.3. The Video Overlay interface

The Video Overlay interface was created to solve the problem of embedding video streams in an application window. The application provides an window handle to the element implementing this interface to draw on, and the element will then use this window handle to draw on rather than creating a new toplevel window. This is useful to embed video in video players.

This interface is implemented by, amongst others, the Video4linux2 elements and by ximagesink, xvimagesink and sdlvideosink.

Chapter 14. Clocks and synchronization in GStreamer

When playing complex media, each sound and video sample must be played in a specific order at a specific time. For this purpose, GStreamer provides a synchronization mechanism.

GStreamer provides support for the following use cases:

- Non-live sources with access faster than playback rate. This is the case where one is reading media from a file and playing it back in a synchronized fashion. In this case, multiple streams need to be synchronized, like audio, video and subtitles.

- Capture and synchronized muxing/mixing of media from multiple live sources. This is a typical use case where you record audio and video from a microphone/camera and mux it into a file for storage.

- Streaming from (slow) network streams with buffering. This is the typical web streaming case where you access content from a streaming server with http.

- Capture from live source and and playback to live source with configurable latency. This is used when, for example, capture from a camera, apply an effect and display the result. It is also used when streaming low latency content over a network with UDP.

- Simultaneous live capture and playback from prerecorded content. This is used in audio recording cases where you play a previously recorded audio and record new samples, the purpose is to have the new audio perfectly in sync with the previously recorded data.

GStreamer uses a `GstClock` object, buffer timestamps and a SEGMENT event to synchronize streams in a pipeline as we will see in the next sections.

14.1. Clock running-time

In a typical computer, there are many sources that can be used as a time source, e.g., the system time, soundcards, CPU performance counters, ... For this reason, there are many `GstClock` implementations available in GStreamer. The clock time doesn't always start from 0 or from some known value. Some clocks start counting from some known start date, other clocks start counting since last reboot, etc...

A `GstClock` returns the **absolute-time** according to that clock with `gst_clock_get_time ()`. The absolute-time (or clock time) of a clock is monotonically increasing. From the absolute-time is a **running-time** calculated, which is simply the difference between a previous snapshot of the absolute-time called the **base-time**. So:

running-time = absolute-time - base-time

A GStreamer `GstPipeline` object maintains a `GstClock` object and a base-time when it goes to the PLAYING state. The pipeline gives a handle to the selected `GstClock` to each element in the pipeline along with selected base-time. The pipeline will select a base-time in such a way that the running-time reflects the total time spent in the PLAYING state. As a result, when the pipeline is PAUSED, the running-time stands still.

Because all objects in the pipeline have the same clock and base-time, they can thus all calculate the running-time according to the pipeline clock.

14.2. Buffer running-time

To calculate a buffer running-time, we need a buffer timestamp and the SEGMENT event that preceeded the buffer. First we can convert the SEGMENT event into a `GstSegment` object and then we can use the `gst_segment_to_running_time ()` function to perform the calculation of the buffer running-time.

Synchronization is now a matter of making sure that a buffer with a certain running-time is played when the clock reaches the same running-time. Usually this task is done by sink elements. Sink also have to take into account the latency configured in the pipeline and add this to the buffer running-time before synchronizing to the pipeline clock.

Non-live sources timestamp buffers with a running-time starting from 0. After a flushing seek, they will produce buffers again from a running-time of 0.

Live sources need to timestamp buffers with a running-time matching the pipeline running-time when the first byte of the buffer was captured.

14.3. Buffer stream-time

The buffer stream-time, also known as the position in the stream, is calculated from the buffer timestamps and the preceding SEGMENT event. It represents the time inside the media as a value between 0 and the total duration of the media.

The stream-time is used in:

• Report the current position in the stream with the POSITION query.

• The position used in the seek events and queries.

• The position used to synchronize controlled values.

The stream-time is never used to synchronize streams, this is only done with the running-time.

14.4. Time overview

Here is an overview of the various timelines used in GStreamer.

The image below represents the different times in the pipeline when playing a 100ms sample and repeating the part between 50ms and 100ms.

Figure 14-1. GStreamer clock and various times

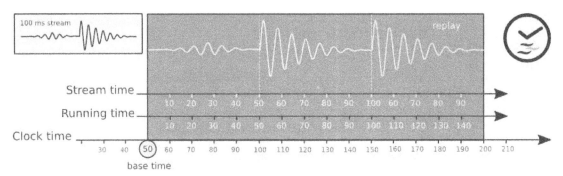

You can see how the running-time of a buffer always increments monotonically along with the clock-time. Buffers are played when their running-time is equal to the clock-time - base-time. The stream-time represents the position in the stream and jumps backwards when repeating.

14.5. Clock providers

A clock provider is an element in the pipeline that can provide a `GstClock` object. The clock object needs to report an absolute-time that is monotonically increasing when the element is in the PLAYING state. It is allowed to pause the clock while the element is PAUSED.

Clock providers exist because they play back media at some rate, and this rate is not necessarily the same as the system clock rate. For example, a soundcard may playback at 44,1 kHz, but that doesn't mean that after *exactly* 1 second *according to the system clock*, the soundcard has played back 44.100 samples. This is only true by approximation. In fact, the audio device has an internal clock based on the number of samples played that we can expose.

If an element with an internal clock needs to synchronize, it needs to estimate when a time according to the pipeline clock will take place according to the internal clock. To estimate this, it needs to slave its clock to the pipeline clock.

If the pipeline clock is exactly the internal clock of an element, the element can skip the slaving step and directly use the pipeline clock to schedule playback. This can be both faster and more accurate.

Therefore, generally, elements with an internal clock like audio input or output devices will be a clock provider for the pipeline.

When the pipeline goes to the PLAYING state, it will go over all elements in the pipeline from sink to source and ask each element if they can provide a clock. The last element that can provide a clock will be used as the clock provider in the pipeline. This algorithm prefers a clock from an audio sink in a typical playback pipeline and a clock from source elements in a typical capture pipeline.

There exist some bus messages to let you know about the clock and clock providers in the pipeline. You can see what clock is selected in the pipeline by looking at the NEW_CLOCK message on the bus. When a clock provider is removed from the pipeline, a CLOCK_LOST message is posted and the application should go to PAUSED and back to PLAYING to select a new clock.

14.6. Latency

The latency is the time it takes for a sample captured at timestamp X to reach the sink. This time is measured against the clock in the pipeline. For pipelines where the only elements that synchronize against the clock are the sinks, the latency is always 0 since no other element is delaying the buffer.

For pipelines with live sources, a latency is introduced, mostly because of the way a live source works. Consider an audio source, it will start capturing the first sample at time 0. If the source pushes buffers with 44100 samples at a time at 44100Hz it will have collected the buffer at second 1. Since the timestamp of the buffer is 0 and the time of the clock is now >= 1 second, the sink will drop this buffer because it is too late. Without any latency compensation in the sink, all buffers will be dropped.

14.6.1. Latency compensation

Before the pipeline goes to the PLAYING state, it will, in addition to selecting a clock and calculating a base-time, calculate the latency in the pipeline. It does this by doing a LATENCY query on all the sinks in the pipeline. The pipeline then selects the maximum latency in the pipeline and configures this with a LATENCY event.

All sink elements will delay playback by the value in the LATENCY event. Since all sinks delay with the same amount of time, they will be relative in sync.

14.6.2. Dynamic Latency

Adding/removing elements to/from a pipeline or changing element properties can change the latency in a pipeline. An element can request a latency change in the pipeline by posting a LATENCY message on the bus. The application can then decide to query and redistribute a new latency or not. Changing the latency in a pipeline might cause visual or audible glitches and should therefore only be done by the application when it is allowed.

Chapter 15. Buffering

The purpose of buffering is to accumulate enough data in a pipeline so that playback can occur smoothly and without interruptions. It is typically done when reading from a (slow) and non-live network source but can also be used for live sources.

GStreamer provides support for the following use cases:

- Buffering up to a specific amount of data, in memory, before starting playback so that network fluctuations are minimized. See Section 15.1.

- Download of the network file to a local disk with fast seeking in the downloaded data. This is similar to the quicktime/youtube players. See Section 15.2.

- Caching of (semi)-live streams to a local, on disk, ringbuffer with seeking in the cached area. This is similar to tivo-like timeshifting. See Section 15.3.

GStreamer can provide the application with progress reports about the current buffering state as well as let the application decide on how to buffer and when the buffering stops.

In the most simple case, the application has to listen for BUFFERING messages on the bus. If the percent indicator inside the BUFFERING message is smaller than 100, the pipeline is buffering. When a message is received with 100 percent, buffering is complete. In the buffering state, the application should keep the pipeline in the PAUSED state. When buffering completes, it can put the pipeline (back) in the PLAYING state.

What follows is an example of how the message handler could deal with the BUFFERING messages. We will see more advanced methods in Section 15.5.

```
[...]

switch (GST_MESSAGE_TYPE (message)) {
  case GST_MESSAGE_BUFFERING:{
    gint percent;

    /* no state management needed for live pipelines */
    if (is_live)
      break;

    gst_message_parse_buffering (message, &percent);

    if (percent == 100) {
      /* a 100% message means buffering is done */
      buffering = FALSE;
      /* if the desired state is playing, go back */
```

```
      if (target_state == GST_STATE_PLAYING) {
        gst_element_set_state (pipeline, GST_STATE_PLAYING);
      }
    } else {
      /* buffering busy */
      if (!buffering && target_state == GST_STATE_PLAYING) {
        /* we were not buffering but PLAYING, PAUSE  the pipeline. */
        gst_element_set_state (pipeline, GST_STATE_PAUSED);
      }
      buffering = TRUE;
    }
    break;
  case ...

[...]
```

15.1. Stream buffering

```
+---------+      +---------+      +-------+
| httpsrc |      | buffer  |      | demux |
|      src - sink       src - sink     ....
+---------+      +---------+      +-------+
```

In this case we are reading from a slow network source into a buffer element (such as queue2).

The buffer element has a low and high watermark expressed in bytes. The buffer uses the watermarks as follows:

• The buffer element will post BUFFERING messages until the high watermark is hit. This instructs the application to keep the pipeline PAUSED, which will eventually block the srcpad from pushing while data is prerolled in the sinks.

• When the high watermark is hit, a BUFFERING message with 100% will be posted, which instructs the application to continue playback.

• When during playback, the low watermark is hit, the queue will start posting BUFFERING messages again, making the application PAUSE the pipeline again until the high watermark is hit again. This is called the rebuffering stage.

• During playback, the queue level will fluctuate between the high and the low watermark as a way to compensate for network irregularities.

This buffering method is usable when the demuxer operates in push mode. Seeking in the stream requires the seek to happen in the network source. It is mostly desirable when the total duration of the file is not known, such as in live streaming or when efficient seeking is not possible/required.

The problem is configuring a good low and high watermark. Here are some ideas:

- It is possible to measure the network bandwidth and configure the low/high watermarks in such a way that buffering takes a fixed amount of time.

  The queue2 element in GStreamer core has the max-size-time property that, together with the use-rate-estimate property, does exactly that. Also the playbin buffer-duration property uses the rate estimate to scale the amount of data that is buffered.

- Based on the codec bitrate, it is also possible to set the watermarks in such a way that a fixed amount of data is buffered before playback starts. Normally, the buffering element doesn't know about the bitrate of the stream but it can get this with a query.

- Start with a fixed amount of bytes, measure the time between rebuffering and increase the queue size until the time between rebuffering is within the application's chosen limits.

The buffering element can be inserted anywhere in the pipeline. You could, for example, insert the buffering element before a decoder. This would make it possible to set the low/high watermarks based on time.

The buffering flag on playbin, performs buffering on the parsed data. Another advantage of doing the buffering at a later stage is that you can let the demuxer operate in pull mode. When reading data from a slow network drive (with filesrc) this can be an interesting way to buffer.

15.2. Download buffering

```
+---------+      +---------+      +-------+
| httpsrc |      | buffer  |      | demux |
|     src - sink        src - sink    ....
+---------+      +----|----+      +-------+
                      V
                    file
```

If we know the server is streaming a fixed length file to the client, the application can choose to download the entire file on disk. The buffer element will provide a push or pull based srcpad to the demuxer to navigate in the downloaded file.

This mode is only suitable when the client can determine the length of the file on the server.

In this case, buffering messages will be emitted as usual when the requested range is not within the downloaded area + buffersize. The buffering message will also contain an indication that incremental download is being performed. This flag can be used to let the application control the buffering in a more intelligent way, using the BUFFERING query, for example. See Section 15.5.

15.3. Timeshift buffering

```
+---------+        +---------+        +-------+
| httpsrc |        | buffer  |        | demux |
|       src - sink        src - sink        ....
+---------+        +----|----+        +-------+
                        v
                  file-ringbuffer
```

In this mode, a fixed size ringbuffer is kept to download the server content. This allows for seeking in the buffered data. Depending on the size of the ringbuffer one can seek further back in time.

This mode is suitable for all live streams. As with the incremental download mode, buffering messages are emitted along with an indication that timeshifting download is in progress.

15.4. Live buffering

In live pipelines we usually introduce some fixed latency between the capture and the playback elements. This latency can be introduced by a queue (such as a jitterbuffer) or by other means (in the audiosink).

Buffering messages can be emitted in those live pipelines as well and serve as an indication to the user of the latency buffering. The application usually does not react to these buffering messages with a state change.

15.5. Buffering strategies

What follows are some ideas for implementing different buffering strategies based on the buffering messages and buffering query.

15.5.1. No-rebuffer strategy

We would like to buffer enough data in the pipeline so that playback continues without interruptions. What we need to know to implement this is know the total remaining playback time in the file and the total remaining download time. If the buffering time is less than the playback time, we can start playback without interruptions.

We have all this information available with the DURATION, POSITION and BUFFERING queries. We need to periodically execute the buffering query to get the current buffering status. We also need to have a large enough buffer to hold the complete file, worst case. It is best to use this buffering strategy with download buffering (see Section 15.2).

This is what the code would look like:

```
#include <gst/gst.h>

GstState target_state;
static gboolean is_live;
static gboolean is_buffering;

static gboolean
buffer_timeout (gpointer data)
{
  GstElement *pipeline = data;
  GstQuery *query;
  gboolean busy;
  gint percent;
  gint64 estimated_total;
  gint64 position, duration;
  guint64 play_left;

  query = gst_query_new_buffering (GST_FORMAT_TIME);

  if (!gst_element_query (pipeline, query))
    return TRUE;

  gst_query_parse_buffering_percent (query, &busy, &percent);
  gst_query_parse_buffering_range (query, NULL, NULL, NULL, &estimated_total);

  if (estimated_total == -1)
    estimated_total = 0;

  /* calculate the remaining playback time */
  if (!gst_element_query_position (pipeline, GST_FORMAT_TIME, &position))
    position = -1;
  if (!gst_element_query_duration (pipeline, GST_FORMAT_TIME, &duration))
    duration = -1;

  if (duration != -1 && position != -1)
    play_left = GST_TIME_AS_MSECONDS (duration - position);
  else
    play_left = 0;

  g_message ("play_left %" G_GUINT64_FORMAT", estimated_total %" G_GUINT64_FORMAT
      ", percent %d", play_left, estimated_total, percent);

  /* we are buffering or the estimated download time is bigger than the
   * remaining playback time. We keep buffering. */
  is_buffering = (busy || estimated_total * 1.1 > play_left);
```

```
  if (!is_buffering)
    gst_element_set_state (pipeline, target_state);

  return is_buffering;
}

static void
on_message_buffering (GstBus *bus, GstMessage *message, gpointer user_data)
{
  GstElement *pipeline = user_data;
  gint percent;

  /* no state management needed for live pipelines */
  if (is_live)
    return;

  gst_message_parse_buffering (message, &percent);

  if (percent < 100) {
    /* buffering busy */
    if (!is_buffering) {
      is_buffering = TRUE;
      if (target_state == GST_STATE_PLAYING) {
        /* we were not buffering but PLAYING, PAUSE  the pipeline. */
        gst_element_set_state (pipeline, GST_STATE_PAUSED);
      }
    }
  }
}

static void
on_message_async_done (GstBus *bus, GstMessage *message, gpointer user_data)
{
  GstElement *pipeline = user_data;

  if (!is_buffering)
    gst_element_set_state (pipeline, target_state);
  else
    g_timeout_add (500, buffer_timeout, pipeline);
}

gint
main (gint   argc,
      gchar *argv[])
{
  GstElement *pipeline;
  GMainLoop *loop;
  GstBus *bus;
  GstStateChangeReturn ret;

  /* init GStreamer */
  gst_init (&amp;argc, &amp;argv);
```

```
loop = g_main_loop_new (NULL, FALSE);

/* make sure we have a URI */
if (argc != 2) {
  g_print ("Usage: %s &lt;URI&gt;\n", argv[0]);
  return -1;
}

/* set up */
pipeline = gst_element_factory_make ("playbin", "pipeline");
g_object_set (G_OBJECT (pipeline), "uri", argv[1], NULL);
g_object_set (G_OBJECT (pipeline), "flags", 0x697 , NULL);

bus = gst_pipeline_get_bus (GST_PIPELINE (pipeline));
gst_bus_add_signal_watch (bus);

g_signal_connect (bus, "message::buffering",
  (GCallback) on_message_buffering, pipeline);
g_signal_connect (bus, "message::async-done",
  (GCallback) on_message_async_done, pipeline);
gst_object_unref (bus);

is_buffering = FALSE;
target_state = GST_STATE_PLAYING;
ret = gst_element_set_state (pipeline, GST_STATE_PAUSED);

switch (ret) {
  case GST_STATE_CHANGE_SUCCESS:
    is_live = FALSE;
    break;

  case GST_STATE_CHANGE_FAILURE:
    g_warning ("failed to PAUSE");
    return -1;

  case GST_STATE_CHANGE_NO_PREROLL:
    is_live = TRUE;
    break;

  default:
    break;
}

/* now run */
g_main_loop_run (loop);

/* also clean up */
gst_element_set_state (pipeline, GST_STATE_NULL);
gst_object_unref (GST_OBJECT (pipeline));
g_main_loop_unref (loop);

return 0;
}
```

See how we set the pipeline to the PAUSED state first. We will receive buffering messages during the preroll state when buffering is needed. When we are prerolled (on_message_async_done) we see if buffering is going on, if not, we start playback. If buffering was going on, we start a timeout to poll the buffering state. If the estimated time to download is less than the remaining playback time, we start playback.

Chapter 16. Dynamic Controllable Parameters

16.1. Getting Started

The controller subsystem offers a lightweight way to adjust gobject properties over stream-time. Normally these properties are changed using `g_object_set()`. Timing those calls reliably so that the changes affect certain stream times is close to impossible. The controller takes time into account. It works by attaching control-sources to properties using control-bindings. Control-sources provide values for a given time-stamp that are usually in the range of 0.0 to 1.0. Control-bindings map the control-value to a gobject property they are bound to - converting the type and scaling to the target property value range. At run-time the elements continuously pull values changes for the current stream-time to update the gobject properties. GStreamer includes a few different control-sources and control-bindings already, but applications can define their own by sub-classing from the respective base classes.

Most parts of the controller mechanism is implemented in GstObject. Also the base classes for control-sources and control-bindings are included in the core library. The existing implementations are contained within the `gstcontroller` library. You need to include the header in your application's source file:

```
...
#include <gst/gst.h>
#include <gst/controller/gstinterpolationcontrolsource.h>
#include <gst/controller/gstdirectcontrolbinding.h>
...
```

Your application should link to the shared library `gstreamer-controller`. One can get the required flag for compiler and linker by using pkg-config for gstreamer-controller-1.0.

16.2. Setting up parameter control

If we have our pipeline set up and want to control some parameters, we first need to create a control-source. Lets use an interpolation control-source:

```
csource = gst_interpolation_control_source_new ();
g_object_set (csource, "mode", GST_INTERPOLATION_MODE_LINEAR, NULL);
```

Now we need to attach the control-source to the gobject property. This is done with a control-binding. One control source can be attached to several object properties (even in different objects) using separate control-bindings.

```
gst_object_add_control_binding (object, gst_direct_control_binding_new (object, "prop1",
```

This type control-source takes new property values from a list of time-stamped parameter changes. The source can e.g. fill gaps by smoothing parameter changes This behavior can be configured by setting the mode property of the control-source. Other control sources e.g. produce a stream of values by calling `sin()` function. They have parameters to control e.g. the frequency. As control-sources are GstObjects too, one can attach control-sources to these properties too.

Now we can set some control points. These are time-stamped gdouble values and are usually in the range of 0.0 to 1.0. A value of 1.0 is later mapped to the maximum value in the target properties value range. The values become active when the timestamp is reached. They still stay in the list. If e.g. the pipeline runs a loop (using a segmented seek), the control-curve gets repeated as well.

```
GstTimedValueControlSource *tv_csource = (GstTimedValueControlSource *)csource;
gst_timed_value_control_source_set (tv_csource, 0 * GST_SECOND, 0.0);
gst_timed_value_control_source_set (tv_csource, 1 * GST_SECOND, 1.0);
```

Now everything is ready to play. If the control-source is e.g. bound to a volume property, we will head a fade-in over 1 second. One word of caution, the volume element that comes with gstreamer has a value range of 0.0 to 4.0 on its volume property. If the above control-source is attached to the property the volume will ramp up to 400%!

One final note - the controller subsystem has a built-in live-mode. Even though a property has a control-source assigned one can change the GObject property through the `g_object_set()`. This is highly useful when binding the GObject properties to GUI widgets. When the user adjusts the value with the widget, one can set the GObject property and this remains active until the next programmed control-source value overrides it. This also works with smoothed parameters. It does not work for control-sources that constantly update the property (e.g. the lfo_control_source).

Chapter 17. Threads

GStreamer is inherently multi-threaded, and is fully thread-safe. Most threading internals are hidden from the application, which should make application development easier. However, in some cases, applications may want to have influence on some parts of those. GStreamer allows applications to force the use of multiple threads over some parts of a pipeline. See Section 17.3.

GStreamer can also notify you when threads are created so that you can configure things such as the thread priority or the threadpool to use. See Section 17.2.

17.1. Scheduling in GStreamer

Each element in the GStreamer pipeline decides how it is going to be scheduled. Elements can choose if their pads are to be scheduled push-based or pull-based. An element can, for example, choose to start a thread to start pulling from the sink pad or/and start pushing on the source pad. An element can also choose to use the upstream or downstream thread for its data processing in push and pull mode respectively. GStreamer does not pose any restrictions on how the element chooses to be scheduled. See the Plugin Writer Guide for more details.

What will happen in any case is that some elements will start a thread for their data processing, called the "streaming threads". The streaming threads, or `GstTask` objects, are created from a `GstTaskPool` when the element needs to make a streaming thread. In the next section we see how we can receive notifications of the tasks and pools.

17.2. Configuring Threads in GStreamer

A STREAM_STATUS message is posted on the bus to inform you about the status of the streaming threads. You will get the following information from the message:

- When a new thread is about to be created, you will be notified of this with a GST_STREAM_STATUS_TYPE_CREATE type. It is then possible to configure a `GstTaskPool` in the `GstTask`. The custom taskpool will provide custom threads for the task to implement the streaming threads.

  This message needs to be handled synchronously if you want to configure a custom taskpool. If you don't configure the taskpool on the task when this message returns, the task will use its default pool.

- When a thread is entered or left. This is the moment where you could configure thread priorities. You also get a notification when a thread is destroyed.

• You get messages when the thread starts, pauses and stops. This could be used to visualize the status of streaming threads in a gui application.

We will now look at some examples in the next sections.

17.2.1. Boost priority of a thread

```
.----------.      .----------.
| faksesrc |      | fakesink |
|          src->sink         |
'----------'      '----------'
```

Let's look at the simple pipeline above. We would like to boost the priority of the streaming thread. It will be the fakesrc element that starts the streaming thread for generating the fake data pushing them to the peer fakesink. The flow for changing the priority would go like this:

• When going from READY to PAUSED state, fakesrc will require a streaming thread for pushing data into the fakesink. It will post a STREAM_STATUS message indicating its requirement for a streaming thread.

• The application will react to the STREAM_STATUS messages with a sync bus handler. It will then configure a custom `GstTaskPool` on the `GstTask` inside the message. The custom taskpool is responsible for creating the threads. In this example we will make a thread with a higher priority.

• Alternatively, since the sync message is called in the thread context, you can use thread ENTER/LEAVE notifications to change the priority or scheduling pollicy of the current thread.

In a first step we need to implement a custom `GstTaskPool` that we can configure on the task. Below is the implementation of a `GstTaskPool` subclass that uses pthreads to create a SCHED_RR real-time thread. Note that creating real-time threads might require extra priveleges.

```
#include <pthread.h>

typedef struct
{
  pthread_t thread;
} TestRTId;

G_DEFINE_TYPE (TestRTPool, test_rt_pool, GST_TYPE_TASK_POOL);
```

```
static void
default_prepare (GstTaskPool * pool, GError ** error)
{
  /* we don't do anything here. We could construct a pool of threads here that
   * we could reuse later but we don't */
}

static void
default_cleanup (GstTaskPool * pool)
{
}

static gpointer
default_push (GstTaskPool * pool, GstTaskPoolFunction func, gpointer data,
    GError ** error)
{
  TestRTId *tid;
  gint res;
  pthread_attr_t attr;
  struct sched_param param;

  tid = g_slice_new0 (TestRTId);

  pthread_attr_init (&attr);
  if ((res = pthread_attr_setschedpolicy (&attr, SCHED_RR)) != 0)
    g_warning ("setschedpolicy: failure: %p", g_strerror (res));

  param.sched_priority = 50;
  if ((res = pthread_attr_setschedparam (&attr, &param)) != 0)
    g_warning ("setschedparam: failure: %p", g_strerror (res));

  if ((res = pthread_attr_setinheritsched (&attr, PTHREAD_EXPLICIT_SCHED)) != 0)
    g_warning ("setinheritsched: failure: %p", g_strerror (res));

  res = pthread_create (&tid->thread, &attr, (void *(*)(void *)) func, data);

  if (res != 0) {
    g_set_error (error, G_THREAD_ERROR, G_THREAD_ERROR_AGAIN,
        "Error creating thread: %s", g_strerror (res));
    g_slice_free (TestRTId, tid);
    tid = NULL;
  }

  return tid;
}

static void
default_join (GstTaskPool * pool, gpointer id)
{
  TestRTId *tid = (TestRTId *) id;

  pthread_join (tid->thread, NULL);
```

```
   g_slice_free (TestRTId, tid);
}

static void
test_rt_pool_class_init (TestRTPoolClass * klass)
{
  GstTaskPoolClass *gsttaskpool_class;

  gsttaskpool_class = (GstTaskPoolClass *) klass;

  gsttaskpool_class->prepare = default_prepare;
  gsttaskpool_class->cleanup = default_cleanup;
  gsttaskpool_class->push = default_push;
  gsttaskpool_class->join = default_join;
}

static void
test_rt_pool_init (TestRTPool * pool)
{
}

GstTaskPool *
test_rt_pool_new (void)
{
  GstTaskPool *pool;

  pool = g_object_new (TEST_TYPE_RT_POOL, NULL);

  return pool;
}
```

The important function to implement when writing an taskpool is the "push" function. The implementation should start a thread that calls the given function. More involved implementations might want to keep some threads around in a pool because creating and destroying threads is not always the fastest operation.

In a next step we need to actually configure the custom taskpool when the fakesrc needs it. For this we intercept the STREAM_STATUS messages with a sync handler.

```
static GMainLoop* loop;

static void
on_stream_status (GstBus     *bus,
                  GstMessage *message,
                  gpointer    user_data)
{
```

```
      GstStreamStatusType type;
      GstElement *owner;
      const GValue *val;
      GstTask *task = NULL;

      gst_message_parse_stream_status (message, &type, &owner);

      val = gst_message_get_stream_status_object (message);

      /* see if we know how to deal with this object */
      if (G_VALUE_TYPE (val) == GST_TYPE_TASK) {
        task = g_value_get_object (val);
      }

      switch (type) {
        case GST_STREAM_STATUS_TYPE_CREATE:
          if (task) {
            GstTaskPool *pool;

            pool = test_rt_pool_new ();

            gst_task_set_pool (task, pool);
          }
          break;
        default:
          break;
      }
    }

static void
on_error (GstBus     *bus,
          GstMessage *message,
          gpointer    user_data)
{
  g_message ("received ERROR");
  g_main_loop_quit (loop);
}

static void
on_eos (GstBus     *bus,
        GstMessage *message,
        gpointer    user_data)
{
  g_main_loop_quit (loop);
}

int
main (int argc, char *argv[])
{
  GstElement *bin, *fakesrc, *fakesink;
  GstBus *bus;
  GstStateChangeReturn ret;
```

```
gst_init (&argc, &argv);

/* create a new bin to hold the elements */
bin = gst_pipeline_new ("pipeline");
g_assert (bin);

/* create a source */
fakesrc = gst_element_factory_make ("fakesrc", "fakesrc");
g_assert (fakesrc);
g_object_set (fakesrc, "num-buffers", 50, NULL);

/* and a sink */
fakesink = gst_element_factory_make ("fakesink", "fakesink");
g_assert (fakesink);

/* add objects to the main pipeline */
gst_bin_add_many (GST_BIN (bin), fakesrc, fakesink, NULL);

/* link the elements */
gst_element_link (fakesrc, fakesink);

loop = g_main_loop_new (NULL, FALSE);

/* get the bus, we need to install a sync handler */
bus = gst_pipeline_get_bus (GST_PIPELINE (bin));
gst_bus_enable_sync_message_emission (bus);
gst_bus_add_signal_watch (bus);

g_signal_connect (bus, "sync-message::stream-status",
    (GCallback) on_stream_status, NULL);
g_signal_connect (bus, "message::error",
    (GCallback) on_error, NULL);
g_signal_connect (bus, "message::eos",
    (GCallback) on_eos, NULL);

/* start playing */
ret = gst_element_set_state (bin, GST_STATE_PLAYING);
if (ret != GST_STATE_CHANGE_SUCCESS) {
  g_message ("failed to change state");
  return -1;
}

/* Run event loop listening for bus messages until EOS or ERROR */
g_main_loop_run (loop);

/* stop the bin */
gst_element_set_state (bin, GST_STATE_NULL);
gst_object_unref (bus);
g_main_loop_unref (loop);

return 0;
}
```

Note that this program likely needs root permissions in order to create real-time threads. When the thread can't be created, the state change function will fail, which we catch in the application above.

When there are multiple threads in the pipeline, you will receive multiple STREAM_STATUS messages. You should use the owner of the message, which is likely the pad or the element that starts the thread, to figure out what the function of this thread is in the context of the application.

17.3. When would you want to force a thread?

We have seen that threads are created by elements but it is also possible to insert elements in the pipeline for the sole purpose of forcing a new thread in the pipeline.

There are several reasons to force the use of threads. However, for performance reasons, you never want to use one thread for every element out there, since that will create some overhead. Let's now list some situations where threads can be particularly useful:

- Data buffering, for example when dealing with network streams or when recording data from a live stream such as a video or audio card. Short hickups elsewhere in the pipeline will not cause data loss. See also Section 15.1 about network buffering with queue2.

Figure 17-1. Data buffering, from a networked source

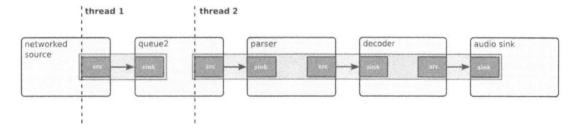

- Synchronizing output devices, e.g. when playing a stream containing both video and audio data. By using threads for both outputs, they will run independently and their synchronization will be better.

Figure 17-2. Synchronizing audio and video sinks

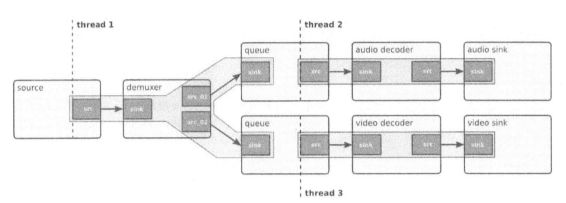

Above, we've mentioned the "queue" element several times now. A queue is the thread boundary element through which you can force the use of threads. It does so by using a classic provider/consumer model as learned in threading classes at universities all around the world. By doing this, it acts both as a means to make data throughput between threads threadsafe, and it can also act as a buffer. Queues have several `GObject` properties to be configured for specific uses. For example, you can set lower and upper thresholds for the element. If there's less data than the lower threshold (default: disabled), it will block output. If there's more data than the upper threshold, it will block input or (if configured to do so) drop data.

To use a queue (and therefore force the use of two distinct threads in the pipeline), one can simply create a "queue" element and put this in as part of the pipeline. GStreamer will take care of all threading details internally.

Chapter 18. Autoplugging

In Chapter 10, you've learned to build a simple media player for Ogg/Vorbis files. By using alternative elements, you are able to build media players for other media types, such as Ogg/Speex, MP3 or even video formats. However, you would rather want to build an application that can automatically detect the media type of a stream and automatically generate the best possible pipeline by looking at all available elements in a system. This process is called autoplugging, and GStreamer contains high-quality autopluggers. If you're looking for an autoplugger, don't read any further and go to Chapter 20. This chapter will explain the *concept* of autoplugging and typefinding. It will explain what systems GStreamer includes to dynamically detect the type of a media stream, and how to generate a pipeline of decoder elements to playback this media. The same principles can also be used for transcoding. Because of the full dynamicity of this concept, GStreamer can be automatically extended to support new media types without needing any adaptations to its autopluggers.

We will first introduce the concept of Media types as a dynamic and extendible way of identifying media streams. After that, we will introduce the concept of typefinding to find the type of a media stream. Lastly, we will explain how autoplugging and the GStreamer registry can be used to setup a pipeline that will convert media from one mediatype to another, for example for media decoding.

18.1. Media types as a way to identify streams

We have previously introduced the concept of capabilities as a way for elements (or, rather, pads) to agree on a media type when streaming data from one element to the next (see Section 8.2). We have explained that a capability is a combination of a media type and a set of properties. For most container formats (those are the files that you will find on your hard disk; Ogg, for example, is a container format), no properties are needed to describe the stream. Only a media type is needed. A full list of media types and accompanying properties can be found in the Plugin Writer's Guide (http://gstreamer.freedesktop.org/data/doc/gstreamer/head/pwg/html/section-types-definitions.html).

An element must associate a media type to its source and sink pads when it is loaded into the system. GStreamer knows about the different elements and what type of data they expect and emit through the GStreamer registry. This allows for very dynamic and extensible element creation as we will see.

In Chapter 10, we've learned to build a music player for Ogg/Vorbis files. Let's look at the media types associated with each pad in this pipeline. Figure 18-1 shows what media type belongs to each pad in this pipeline.

Figure 18-1. The Hello world pipeline with media types

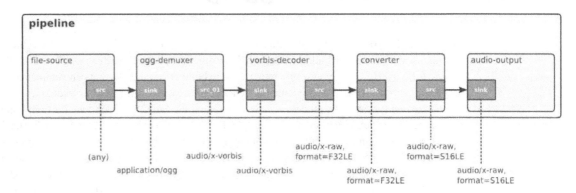

Now that we have an idea how GStreamer identifies known media streams, we can look at methods GStreamer uses to setup pipelines for media handling and for media type detection.

18.2. Media stream type detection

Usually, when loading a media stream, the type of the stream is not known. This means that before we can choose a pipeline to decode the stream, we first need to detect the stream type. GStreamer uses the concept of typefinding for this. Typefinding is a normal part of a pipeline, it will read data for as long as the type of a stream is unknown. During this period, it will provide data to all plugins that implement a typefinder. When one of the typefinders recognizes the stream, the typefind element will emit a signal and act as a passthrough module from that point on. If no type was found, it will emit an error and further media processing will stop.

Once the typefind element has found a type, the application can use this to plug together a pipeline to decode the media stream. This will be discussed in the next section.

Plugins in GStreamer can, as mentioned before, implement typefinder functionality. A plugin implementing this functionality will submit a media type, optionally a set of file extensions commonly used for this media type, and a typefind function. Once this typefind function inside the plugin is called, the plugin will see if the data in this media stream matches a specific pattern that marks the media type identified by that media type. If it does, it will notify the typefind element of this fact, telling which mediatype was recognized and how certain we are that this stream is indeed that mediatype. Once this run has been completed for all plugins implementing a typefind functionality, the typefind element will tell the application what kind of media stream it thinks to have recognized.

The following code should explain how to use the typefind element. It will print the detected media type, or tell that the media type was not found. The next section will introduce more useful behaviours, such as plugging together a decoding pipeline.

```
#include <gst/gst.h>
```

```
[.. my_bus_callback goes here ..]

static gboolean
idle_exit_loop (gpointer data)
{
  g_main_loop_quit ((GMainLoop *) data);

  /* once */
  return FALSE;
}

static void
cb_typefound (GstElement *typefind,
      guint       probability,
      GstCaps    *caps,
      gpointer    data)
{
  GMainLoop *loop = data;
  gchar *type;

  type = gst_caps_to_string (caps);
  g_print ("Media type %s found, probability %d%%\n", type, probability);
  g_free (type);

  /* since we connect to a signal in the pipeline thread context, we need
   * to set an idle handler to exit the main loop in the mainloop context.
   * Normally, your app should not need to worry about such things. */
  g_idle_add (idle_exit_loop, loop);
}

gint
main (gint   argc,
      gchar *argv[])
{
  GMainLoop *loop;
  GstElement *pipeline, *filesrc, *typefind, *fakesink;
  GstBus *bus;

  /* init GStreamer */
  gst_init (&argc, &argv);
  loop = g_main_loop_new (NULL, FALSE);

  /* check args */
  if (argc != 2) {
    g_print ("Usage: %s <filename>\n", argv[0]);
    return -1;
  }

  /* create a new pipeline to hold the elements */
  pipeline = gst_pipeline_new ("pipe");

  bus = gst_pipeline_get_bus (GST_PIPELINE (pipeline));
```

```
gst_bus_add_watch (bus, my_bus_callback, NULL);
gst_object_unref (bus);

/* create file source and typefind element */
filesrc = gst_element_factory_make ("filesrc", "source");
g_object_set (G_OBJECT (filesrc), "location", argv[1], NULL);
typefind = gst_element_factory_make ("typefind", "typefinder");
g_signal_connect (typefind, "have-type", G_CALLBACK (cb_typefound), loop);
fakesink = gst_element_factory_make ("fakesink", "sink");

/* setup */
gst_bin_add_many (GST_BIN (pipeline), filesrc, typefind, fakesink, NULL);
gst_element_link_many (filesrc, typefind, fakesink, NULL);
gst_element_set_state (GST_ELEMENT (pipeline), GST_STATE_PLAYING);
g_main_loop_run (loop);

/* unset */
gst_element_set_state (GST_ELEMENT (pipeline), GST_STATE_NULL);
gst_object_unref (GST_OBJECT (pipeline));

return 0;
}
```

Once a media type has been detected, you can plug an element (e.g. a demuxer or decoder) to the source pad of the typefind element, and decoding of the media stream will start right after.

18.3. Dynamically autoplugging a pipeline

See Chapter 20 for using the high level object that you can use to dynamically construct pipelines.

Chapter 19. Pipeline manipulation

This chapter will discuss how you can manipulate your pipeline in several ways from your application on. Parts of this chapter are very lowlevel, so be assured that you'll need some programming knowledge and a good understanding of GStreamer before you start reading this.

Topics that will be discussed here include how you can insert data into a pipeline from your application, how to read data from a pipeline, how to manipulate the pipeline's speed, length, starting point and how to listen to a pipeline's data processing.

19.1. Using probes

Probing is best envisioned as a pad listener. Technically, a probe is nothing more than a callback that can be attached to a pad. You can attach a probe using `gst_pad_add_probe ()`. Similarly, one can use the `gst_pad_remove_probe ()` to remove the callback again. The probe notifies you of any activity that happens on the pad, like buffers, events and queries. You can define what kind of notifications you are interested in when you add the probe.

The probe can notify you of the following activity on pads:

- A buffer is pushed or pulled. You want to specify the GST_PAD_PROBE_TYPE_BUFFER when registering the probe. Because the pad can be scheduled in different ways, it is possible to also specify in what scheduling mode you are interested with the optional GST_PAD_PROBE_TYPE_PUSH and GST_PAD_PROBE_TYPE_PULL flags.

  You can use this probe to inspect, modify or drop the buffer. See Section 19.1.1.

- A bufferlist is pushed. Use the GST_PAD_PROBE_TYPE_BUFFER_LIST when registering the probe.

- An event travels over a pad. Use the GST_PAD_PROBE_TYPE_EVENT_DOWNSTREAM and GST_PAD_PROBE_TYPE_EVENT_UPSTREAM flags to select downstream and upstream events. There is also a convenience GST_PAD_PROBE_TYPE_EVENT_BOTH to be notified of events going both upstream and downstream. By default, flush events do not cause a notification. You need to explicitly enable GST_PAD_PROBE_TYPE_EVENT_FLUSH to receive callbacks from flushing events. Events are always only notified in push mode.

  You can use this probe to inspect, modify or drop the event.

- A query travels over a pad. Use the GST_PAD_PROBE_TYPE_QUERY_DOWNSTREAM and GST_PAD_PROBE_TYPE_QUERY_UPSTREAM flags to select downstream and upstream queries. The convenience GST_PAD_PROBE_TYPE_QUERY_BOTH can also be used to select both

Chapter 19. Pipeline manipulation

directions. Query probes will be notified twice, once when the query travels upstream/downstream and once when the query result is returned. You can select in what stage the callback will be called with the GST_PAD_PROBE_TYPE_PUSH and GST_PAD_PROBE_TYPE_PULL, respectively when the query is performed and when the query result is returned.

You can use this probe to inspect or modify the query. You can also answer the query in the probe callback by placing the result value in the query and by returning GST_PAD_PROBE_DROP from the callback.

- In addition to notifying you of dataflow, you can also ask the probe to block the dataflow when the callback returns. This is called a blocking probe and is activated by specifying the GST_PAD_PROBE_TYPE_BLOCK flag. You can use this flag with the other flags to only block dataflow on selected activity. A pad becomes unblocked again if you remove the probe or when you return GST_PAD_PROBE_REMOVE from the callback. You can let only the currently blocked item pass by returning GST_PAD_PROBE_PASS from the callback, it will block again on the next item.

Blocking probes are used to temporarily block pads because they are unlinked or because you are going to unlink them. If the dataflow is not blocked, the pipeline would go into an error state if data is pushed on an unlinked pad. We will se how to use blocking probes to partially preroll a pipeline. See also Section 19.1.2.

- Be notified when no activity is happening on a pad. You install this probe with the GST_PAD_PROBE_TYPE_IDLE flag. You can specify GST_PAD_PROBE_TYPE_PUSH and/or GST_PAD_PROBE_TYPE_PULL to only be notified depending on the pad scheduling mode. The IDLE probe is also a blocking probe in that it will not let any data pass on the pad for as long as the IDLE probe is installed.

You can use idle probes to dynamically relink a pad. We will see how to use idle probes to replace an element in the pipeline. See also Section 19.4.

19.1.1. Data probes

Data probes allow you to be notified when there is data passing on a pad. When adding the probe, specify the GST_PAD_PROBE_TYPE_BUFFER and/or GST_PAD_PROBE_TYPE_BUFFER_LIST.

Data probes run in pipeline streaming thread context, so callbacks should try to not block and generally not do any weird stuff, since this could have a negative impact on pipeline performance or, in case of bugs, cause deadlocks or crashes. More precisely, one should usually not call any GUI-related functions from within a probe callback, nor try to change the state of the pipeline. An application may post custom messages on the pipeline's bus though to communicate with the main application thread and have it do things like stop the pipeline.

In any case, most common buffer operations that elements can do in _chain () functions, can be done in probe callbacks as well. The example below gives a short impression on how to use them.

```
#include <gst/gst.h>

static GstPadProbeReturn
cb_have_data (GstPad          *pad,
              GstPadProbeInfo *info,
              gpointer          user_data)
{
  gint x, y;
  GstMapInfo map;
  guint16 *ptr, t;
  GstBuffer *buffer;

  buffer = GST_PAD_PROBE_INFO_BUFFER (info);

  buffer = gst_buffer_make_writable (buffer);

  /* Making a buffer writable can fail (for example if it
   * cannot be copied and is used more than once)
   */
  if (buffer == NULL)
    return GST_PAD_PROBE_OK;

  /* Mapping a buffer can fail (non-writable) */
  if (gst_buffer_map (buffer, &map, GST_MAP_WRITE)) {
    ptr = (guint16 *) map.data;
    /* invert data */
    for (y = 0; y < 288; y++) {
      for (x = 0; x < 384 / 2; x++) {
        t = ptr[384 - 1 - x];
        ptr[384 - 1 - x] = ptr[x];
        ptr[x] = t;
      }
      ptr += 384;
    }
    gst_buffer_unmap (buffer, &map);
  }

  GST_PAD_PROBE_INFO_DATA (info) = buffer;

  return GST_PAD_PROBE_OK;
}

gint
main (gint    argc,
      gchar *argv[])
{
  GMainLoop *loop;
  GstElement *pipeline, *src, *sink, *filter, *csp;
```

```
GstCaps *filtercaps;
GstPad *pad;

/* init GStreamer */
gst_init (&argc, &argv);
loop = g_main_loop_new (NULL, FALSE);

/* build */
pipeline = gst_pipeline_new ("my-pipeline");
src = gst_element_factory_make ("videotestsrc", "src");
if (src == NULL)
  g_error ("Could not create 'videotestsrc' element");

filter = gst_element_factory_make ("capsfilter", "filter");
g_assert (filter != NULL); /* should always exist */

csp = gst_element_factory_make ("videoconvert", "csp");
if (csp == NULL)
  g_error ("Could not create 'videoconvert' element");

sink = gst_element_factory_make ("xvimagesink", "sink");
if (sink == NULL) {
  sink = gst_element_factory_make ("ximagesink", "sink");
  if (sink == NULL)
    g_error ("Could not create neither 'xvimagesink' nor 'ximagesink' element");
}

gst_bin_add_many (GST_BIN (pipeline), src, filter, csp, sink, NULL);
gst_element_link_many (src, filter, csp, sink, NULL);
filtercaps = gst_caps_new_simple ("video/x-raw",
 "format", G_TYPE_STRING, "RGB16",
 "width", G_TYPE_INT, 384,
 "height", G_TYPE_INT, 288,
 "framerate", GST_TYPE_FRACTION, 25, 1,
 NULL);
g_object_set (G_OBJECT (filter), "caps", filtercaps, NULL);
gst_caps_unref (filtercaps);

pad = gst_element_get_static_pad (src, "src");
gst_pad_add_probe (pad, GST_PAD_PROBE_TYPE_BUFFER,
    (GstPadProbeCallback) cb_have_data, NULL, NULL);
gst_object_unref (pad);

/* run */
gst_element_set_state (pipeline, GST_STATE_PLAYING);

/* wait until it's up and running or failed */
if (gst_element_get_state (pipeline, NULL, NULL, -1) == GST_STATE_CHANGE_FAILURE) {
  g_error ("Failed to go into PLAYING state");
}

g_print ("Running ...\n");
g_main_loop_run (loop);
```

```
/* exit */
gst_element_set_state (pipeline, GST_STATE_NULL);
gst_object_unref (pipeline);

return 0;
}
```

Compare that output with the output of "gst-launch-1.0 videotestsrc ! xvimagesink", just so you know what you're looking for.

Strictly speaking, a pad probe callback is only allowed to modify the buffer content if the buffer is writable. Whether this is the case or not depends a lot on the pipeline and the elements involved. Often enough, this is the case, but sometimes it is not, and if it is not then unexpected modification of the data or metadata can introduce bugs that are very hard to debug and track down. You can check if a buffer is writable with `gst_buffer_is_writable ()`. Since you can pass back a different buffer than the one passed in, it is a good idea to make the buffer writable in the callback function with `gst_buffer_make_writable ()`.

Pad probes are suited best for looking at data as it passes through the pipeline. If you need to modify data, you should better write your own GStreamer element. Base classes like GstAudioFilter, GstVideoFilter or GstBaseTransform make this fairly easy.

If you just want to inspect buffers as they pass through the pipeline, you don't even need to set up pad probes. You could also just insert an identity element into the pipeline and connect to its "handoff" signal. The identity element also provides a few useful debugging tools like the "dump" property or the "last-message" property (the latter is enabled by passing the '-v' switch to gst-launch and by setting the silent property on the identity to FALSE).

19.1.2. Play a region of a media file

In this example we will show you how to play back a region of a media file. The goal is to only play the part of a file from 2 seconds to 5 seconds and then EOS.

In a first step we will set a uridecodebin element to the PAUSED state and make sure that we block all the source pads that are created. When all the source pads are blocked, we have data on all source pads and we say that the uridecodebin is prerolled.

In a prerolled pipeline we can ask for the duration of the media and we can also perform seeks. We are interested in performing a seek operation on the pipeline to select the range of media that we are interested in.

After we configure the region we are interested in, we can link the sink element, unblock the source pads and set the pipeline to the playing state. You will see that exactly the requested region is played by the sink before it goes to EOS.

What follows is an example application that loosly follows this algorithm.

```
#include <gst/gst.h>

static GMainLoop *loop;
static volatile gint counter;
static GstBus *bus;
static gboolean prerolled = FALSE;
static GstPad *sinkpad;

static void
dec_counter (GstElement * pipeline)
{
  if (prerolled)
    return;

  if (g_atomic_int_dec_and_test (&counter)) {
    /* all probes blocked and no-more-pads signaled, post
     * message on the bus. */
    prerolled = TRUE;

    gst_bus_post (bus, gst_message_new_application (
          GST_OBJECT_CAST (pipeline),
          gst_structure_new_empty ("ExPrerolled")));
  }
}

/* called when a source pad of uridecodebin is blocked */
static GstPadProbeReturn
cb_blocked (GstPad          *pad,
            GstPadProbeInfo *info,
            gpointer         user_data)
{
  GstElement *pipeline = GST_ELEMENT (user_data);

  if (prerolled)
    return GST_PAD_PROBE_REMOVE;

  dec_counter (pipeline);

  return GST_PAD_PROBE_OK;
}

/* called when uridecodebin has a new pad */
static void
cb_pad_added (GstElement *element,
```

```
            GstPad     *pad,
            gpointer   user_data)
{
  GstElement *pipeline = GST_ELEMENT (user_data);

  if (prerolled)
    return;

  g_atomic_int_inc (&counter);

  gst_pad_add_probe (pad, GST_PAD_PROBE_TYPE_BLOCK_DOWNSTREAM,
      (GstPadProbeCallback) cb_blocked, pipeline, NULL);

  /* try to link to the video pad */
  gst_pad_link (pad, sinkpad);
}

/* called when uridecodebin has created all pads */
static void
cb_no_more_pads (GstElement *element,
                 gpointer   user_data)
{
  GstElement *pipeline = GST_ELEMENT (user_data);

  if (prerolled)
    return;

  dec_counter (pipeline);
}

/* called when a new message is posted on the bus */
static void
cb_message (GstBus     *bus,
            GstMessage *message,
            gpointer   user_data)
{
  GstElement *pipeline = GST_ELEMENT (user_data);

  switch (GST_MESSAGE_TYPE (message)) {
    case GST_MESSAGE_ERROR:
      g_print ("we received an error!\n");
      g_main_loop_quit (loop);
      break;
    case GST_MESSAGE_EOS:
      g_print ("we reached EOS\n");
      g_main_loop_quit (loop);
      break;
    case GST_MESSAGE_APPLICATION:
    {
      if (gst_message_has_name (message, "ExPrerolled")) {
        /* it's our message */
        g_print ("we are all prerolled, do seek\n");
        gst_element_seek (pipeline,
```

```
           1.0, GST_FORMAT_TIME,
           GST_SEEK_FLAG_FLUSH | GST_SEEK_FLAG_ACCURATE,
           GST_SEEK_TYPE_SET, 2 * GST_SECOND,
           GST_SEEK_TYPE_SET, 5 * GST_SECOND);

        gst_element_set_state (pipeline, GST_STATE_PLAYING);
      }
      break;
    }
    default:
      break;
  }
}

gint
main (gint   argc,
      gchar *argv[])
{
  GstElement *pipeline, *src, *csp, *vs, *sink;

  /* init GStreamer */
  gst_init (&argc, &argv);
  loop = g_main_loop_new (NULL, FALSE);

  if (argc < 2) {
    g_print ("usage: %s <uri>", argv[0]);
    return -1;
  }

  /* build */
  pipeline = gst_pipeline_new ("my-pipeline");

  bus = gst_pipeline_get_bus (GST_PIPELINE (pipeline));
  gst_bus_add_signal_watch (bus);
  g_signal_connect (bus, "message", (GCallback) cb_message,
      pipeline);

  src = gst_element_factory_make ("uridecodebin", "src");
  if (src == NULL)
    g_error ("Could not create 'uridecodebin' element");

  g_object_set (src, "uri", argv[1], NULL);

  csp = gst_element_factory_make ("videoconvert", "csp");
  if (csp == NULL)
    g_error ("Could not create 'videoconvert' element");

  vs = gst_element_factory_make ("videoscale", "vs");
  if (csp == NULL)
    g_error ("Could not create 'videoscale' element");

  sink = gst_element_factory_make ("autovideosink", "sink");
  if (sink == NULL)
```

```
    g_error ("Could not create 'autovideosink' element");

  gst_bin_add_many (GST_BIN (pipeline), src, csp, vs, sink, NULL);

  /* can't link src yet, it has no pads */
  gst_element_link_many (csp, vs, sink, NULL);

  sinkpad = gst_element_get_static_pad (csp, "sink");

  /* for each pad block that is installed, we will increment
   * the counter. for each pad block that is signaled, we
   * decrement the counter. When the counter is 0 we post
   * an app message to tell the app that all pads are
   * blocked. Start with 1 that is decremented when no-more-pads
   * is signaled to make sure that we only post the message
   * after no-more-pads */
  g_atomic_int_set (&counter, 1);

  g_signal_connect (src, "pad-added",
      (GCallback) cb_pad_added, pipeline);
  g_signal_connect (src, "no-more-pads",
      (GCallback) cb_no_more_pads, pipeline);

  gst_element_set_state (pipeline, GST_STATE_PAUSED);

  g_main_loop_run (loop);

  gst_element_set_state (pipeline, GST_STATE_NULL);

  gst_object_unref (sinkpad);
  gst_object_unref (bus);
  gst_object_unref (pipeline);
  g_main_loop_unref (loop);

  return 0;
}
```

Note that we use a custom application message to signal the main thread that the uridecidebin is prerolled. The main thread will then issue a flushing seek to the requested region. The flush will temporarily unblock the pad and reblock them when new data arrives again. We detect this second block to remove the probes. Then we set the pipeline to PLAYING and it should play from 2 to 5 seconds, then EOS and exit the application.

19.2. Manually adding or removing data from/to a pipeline

Many people have expressed the wish to use their own sources to inject data into a pipeline. Some people have also expressed the wish to grab the output in a pipeline and take care of the actual output inside their application. While either of these methods are strongly discouraged, GStreamer offers support for this. *Beware! You need to know what you are doing.* Since you don't have any support from a base class you need to thoroughly understand state changes and synchronization. If it doesn't work, there are a million ways to shoot yourself in the foot. It's always better to simply write a plugin and have the base class manage it. See the Plugin Writer's Guide for more information on this topic. Also see the next section, which will explain how to embed plugins statically in your application.

There's two possible elements that you can use for the above-mentioned purposes. Those are called "appsrc" (an imaginary source) and "appsink" (an imaginary sink). The same method applies to each of those elements. Here, we will discuss how to use those elements to insert (using appsrc) or grab (using appsink) data from a pipeline, and how to set negotiation.

Both appsrc and appsink provide 2 sets of API. One API uses standard GObject (action) signals and properties. The same API is also available as a regular C api. The C api is more performant but requires you to link to the app library in order to use the elements.

19.2.1. Inserting data with appsrc

First we look at some examples for appsrc, which lets you insert data into the pipeline from the application. Appsrc has some configuration options that define how it will operate. You should decide about the following configurations:

- Will the appsrc operate in push or pull mode. The stream-type property can be used to control this. stream-type of "random-access" will activate pull mode scheduling while the other stream-types activate push mode.

- The caps of the buffers that appsrc will push out. This needs to be configured with the caps property. The caps must be set to a fixed caps and will be used to negotiate a format downstream.

- If the appsrc operates in live mode or not. This can be configured with the is-live property. When operating in live-mode it is important to configure the min-latency and max-latency in appsrc. The min-latency should be set to the amount of time it takes between capturing a buffer and when it is pushed inside appsrc. In live mode, you should timestamp the buffers with the pipeline running-time when the first byte of the buffer was captured before feeding them to appsrc. You can let appsrc do the timestaping with the do-timestamp property (but then the min-latency must be set to 0 because it timestamps based on the running-time when the buffer entered appsrc).

- The format of the SEGMENT event that appsrc will push. The format has implications for how the running-time of the buffers will be calculated so you must be sure you understand this. For live sources you probably want to set the format property to GST_FORMAT_TIME. For non-live source it depends on the media type that you are handling. If you plan to timestamp the buffers, you should probably put a GST_FORMAT_TIME format, otherwise GST_FORMAT_BYTES might be appropriate.

- If appsrc operates in random-access mode, it is important to configure the size property of appsrc with the number of bytes in the stream. This will allow downstream elements to know the size of the media and alows them to seek to the end of the stream when needed.

The main way of handling data to appsrc is by using the function `gst_app_src_push_buffer ()` or by emiting the push-buffer action signal. This will put the buffer onto a queue from which appsrc will read from in its streaming thread. It is important to note that data transport will not happen from the thread that performed the push-buffer call.

The "max-bytes" property controls how much data can be queued in appsrc before appsrc considers the queue full. A filled internal queue will always signal the "enough-data" signal, which signals the application that it should stop pushing data into appsrc. The "block" property will cause appsrc to block the push-buffer method until free data becomes available again.

When the internal queue is running out of data, the "need-data" signal is emitted, which signals the application that it should start pushing more data into appsrc.

In addition to the "need-data" and "enough-data" signals, appsrc can emit the "seek-data" signal when the "stream-mode" property is set to "seekable" or "random-access". The signal argument will contain the new desired position in the stream expressed in the unit set with the "format" property. After receiving the seek-data signal, the application should push-buffers from the new position.

When the last byte is pushed into appsrc, you must call `gst_app_src_end_of_stream ()` to make it send an EOS downstream.

These signals allow the application to operate appsrc in push and pull mode as will be explained next.

19.2.1.1. Using appsrc in push mode

When appsrc is configured in push mode (stream-type is stream or seekable), the application repeatedly calls the push-buffer method with a new buffer. Optionally, the queue size in the appsrc can be controlled with the enough-data and need-data signals by respectively stopping/starting the push-buffer calls. The value of the min-percent property defines how empty the internal appsrc queue needs to be before the need-data signal will be fired. You can set this to some value >0 to avoid completely draining the queue.

When the stream-type is set to seekable, don't forget to implement a seek-data callback.

Use this model when implementing various network protocols or hardware devices.

19.2.1.2. Using appsrc in pull mode

In the pull model, data is fed to appsrc from the need-data signal handler. You should push exactly the amount of bytes requested in the need-data signal. You are only allowed to push less bytes when you are at the end of the stream.

Use this model for file access or other randomly accessible sources.

19.2.1.3. Appsrc example

This example application will generate black/white (it switches every second) video to an Xv-window output by using appsrc as a source with caps to force a format. We use a colorspace conversion element to make sure that we feed the right format to your X server. We configure a video stream with a variable framerate (0/1) and we set the timestamps on the outgoing buffers in such a way that we play 2 frames per second.

Note how we use the pull mode method of pushing new buffers into appsrc although appsrc is running in push mode.

```
#include <gst/gst.h>

static GMainLoop *loop;

static void
cb_need_data (GstElement *appsrc,
      guint       unused_size,
      gpointer    user_data)
{
  static gboolean white = FALSE;
  static GstClockTime timestamp = 0;
  GstBuffer *buffer;
  guint size;
  GstFlowReturn ret;

  size = 385 * 288 * 2;

  buffer = gst_buffer_new_allocate (NULL, size, NULL);

  /* this makes the image black/white */
  gst_buffer_memset (buffer, 0, white ? 0xff : 0x0, size);

  white = !white;

  GST_BUFFER_PTS (buffer) = timestamp;
  GST_BUFFER_DURATION (buffer) = gst_util_uint64_scale_int (1, GST_SECOND, 2);
```

```
    timestamp += GST_BUFFER_DURATION (buffer);

    g_signal_emit_by_name (appsrc, "push-buffer", buffer, &ret);
    gst_buffer_unref (buffer);

    if (ret != GST_FLOW_OK) {
      /* something wrong, stop pushing */
      g_main_loop_quit (loop);
    }
}

gint
main (gint   argc,
      gchar *argv[])
{
  GstElement *pipeline, *appsrc, *conv, *videosink;

  /* init GStreamer */
  gst_init (&argc, &argv);
  loop = g_main_loop_new (NULL, FALSE);

  /* setup pipeline */
  pipeline = gst_pipeline_new ("pipeline");
  appsrc = gst_element_factory_make ("appsrc", "source");
  conv = gst_element_factory_make ("videoconvert", "conv");
  videosink = gst_element_factory_make ("xvimagesink", "videosink");

  /* setup */
  g_object_set (G_OBJECT (appsrc), "caps",
   gst_caps_new_simple ("video/x-raw",
     "format", G_TYPE_STRING, "RGB16",
     "width", G_TYPE_INT, 384,
     "height", G_TYPE_INT, 288,
     "framerate", GST_TYPE_FRACTION, 0, 1,
     NULL), NULL);
  gst_bin_add_many (GST_BIN (pipeline), appsrc, conv, videosink, NULL);
  gst_element_link_many (appsrc, conv, videosink, NULL);

  /* setup appsrc */
  g_object_set (G_OBJECT (appsrc),
"stream-type", 0,
"format", GST_FORMAT_TIME, NULL);
  g_signal_connect (appsrc, "need-data", G_CALLBACK (cb_need_data), NULL);

  /* play */
  gst_element_set_state (pipeline, GST_STATE_PLAYING);
  g_main_loop_run (loop);

  /* clean up */
  gst_element_set_state (pipeline, GST_STATE_NULL);
  gst_object_unref (GST_OBJECT (pipeline));
  g_main_loop_unref (loop);
```

```
return 0;
}
```

19.2.2. Grabbing data with appsink

Unlike appsrc, appsink is a little easier to use. It also supports a pull and push based model of getting data from the pipeline.

The normal way of retrieving samples from appsink is by using the `gst_app_sink_pull_sample()` and `gst_app_sink_pull_preroll()` methods or by using the "pull-sample" and "pull-preroll" signals. These methods block until a sample becomes available in the sink or when the sink is shut down or reaches EOS.

Appsink will internally use a queue to collect buffers from the streaming thread. If the application is not pulling samples fast enough, this queue will consume a lot of memory over time. The "max-buffers" property can be used to limit the queue size. The "drop" property controls whether the streaming thread blocks or if older buffers are dropped when the maximum queue size is reached. Note that blocking the streaming thread can negatively affect real-time performance and should be avoided.

If a blocking behaviour is not desirable, setting the "emit-signals" property to TRUE will make appsink emit the "new-sample" and "new-preroll" signals when a sample can be pulled without blocking.

The "caps" property on appsink can be used to control the formats that appsink can receive. This property can contain non-fixed caps, the format of the pulled samples can be obtained by getting the sample caps.

If one of the pull-preroll or pull-sample methods return NULL, the appsink is stopped or in the EOS state. You can check for the EOS state with the "eos" property or with the `gst_app_sink_is_eos()` method.

The eos signal can also be used to be informed when the EOS state is reached to avoid polling.

Consider configuring the following properties in the appsink:

• The "sync" property if you want to have the sink base class synchronize the buffer against the pipeline clock before handing you the sample.

• Enable Quality-of-Service with the "qos" property. If you are dealing with raw video frames and let the base class sycnhronize on the clock, it might be a good idea to also let the base class send QOS events upstream.

- The caps property that contains the accepted caps. Upstream elements will try to convert the format so that it matches the configured caps on appsink. You must still check the GstSample to get the actual caps of the buffer.

19.2.2.1. Appsink example

What follows is an example on how to capture a snapshot of a video stream using appsink.

```
#include <gst/gst.h>
#ifdef HAVE_GTK
#include <gtk/gtk.h>
#endif

#include <stdlib.h>

#define CAPS "video/x-raw,format=RGB,width=160,pixel-aspect-ratio=1/1"

int
main (int argc, char *argv[])
{
  GstElement *pipeline, *sink;
  gint width, height;
  GstSample *sample;
  gchar *descr;
  GError *error = NULL;
  gint64 duration, position;
  GstStateChangeReturn ret;
  gboolean res;
  GstMapInfo map;

  gst_init (&argc, &argv);

  if (argc != 2) {
    g_print ("usage: %s <uri>\n Writes snapshot.png in the current directory\n",
        argv[0]);
    exit (-1);
  }

  /* create a new pipeline */
  descr =
      g_strdup_printf ("uridecodebin uri=%s ! videoconvert ! videoscale ! "
      " appsink name=sink caps=\"" CAPS "\"", argv[1]);
  pipeline = gst_parse_launch (descr, &error);

  if (error != NULL) {
    g_print ("could not construct pipeline: %s\n", error->message);
    g_clear_error (&error);
    exit (-1);
  }
```

```
/* get sink */
sink = gst_bin_get_by_name (GST_BIN (pipeline), "sink");

/* set to PAUSED to make the first frame arrive in the sink */
ret = gst_element_set_state (pipeline, GST_STATE_PAUSED);
switch (ret) {
  case GST_STATE_CHANGE_FAILURE:
    g_print ("failed to play the file\n");
    exit (-1);
  case GST_STATE_CHANGE_NO_PREROLL:
    /* for live sources, we need to set the pipeline to PLAYING before we can
     * receive a buffer. We don't do that yet */
    g_print ("live sources not supported yet\n");
    exit (-1);
  default:
    break;
}
/* This can block for up to 5 seconds. If your machine is really overloaded,
 * it might time out before the pipeline prerolled and we generate an error. A
 * better way is to run a mainloop and catch errors there. */
ret = gst_element_get_state (pipeline, NULL, NULL, 5 * GST_SECOND);
if (ret == GST_STATE_CHANGE_FAILURE) {
  g_print ("failed to play the file\n");
  exit (-1);
}

/* get the duration */
gst_element_query_duration (pipeline, GST_FORMAT_TIME, &duration);

if (duration != -1)
  /* we have a duration, seek to 5% */
  position = duration * 5 / 100;
else
  /* no duration, seek to 1 second, this could EOS */
  position = 1 * GST_SECOND;

/* seek to the a position in the file. Most files have a black first frame so
 * by seeking to somewhere else we have a bigger chance of getting something
 * more interesting. An optimisation would be to detect black images and then
 * seek a little more */
gst_element_seek_simple (pipeline, GST_FORMAT_TIME,
    GST_SEEK_FLAG_KEY_UNIT | GST_SEEK_FLAG_FLUSH, position);

/* get the preroll buffer from appsink, this block untils appsink really
 * prerolls */
g_signal_emit_by_name (sink, "pull-preroll", &sample, NULL);

/* if we have a buffer now, convert it to a pixbuf. It's possible that we
 * don't have a buffer because we went EOS right away or had an error. */
if (sample) {
  GstBuffer *buffer;
  GstCaps *caps;
```

```
      GstStructure *s;

      /* get the snapshot buffer format now. We set the caps on the appsink so
       * that it can only be an rgb buffer. The only thing we have not specified
       * on the caps is the height, which is dependant on the pixel-aspect-ratio
       * of the source material */
      caps = gst_sample_get_caps (sample);
      if (!caps) {
        g_print ("could not get snapshot format\n");
        exit (-1);
      }
      s = gst_caps_get_structure (caps, 0);

      /* we need to get the final caps on the buffer to get the size */
      res = gst_structure_get_int (s, "width", &width);
      res |= gst_structure_get_int (s, "height", &height);
      if (!res) {
        g_print ("could not get snapshot dimension\n");
        exit (-1);
      }

      /* create pixmap from buffer and save, gstreamer video buffers have a stride
       * that is rounded up to the nearest multiple of 4 */
      buffer = gst_sample_get_buffer (sample);
      /* Mapping a buffer can fail (non-readable) */
      if (gst_buffer_map (buffer, &map, GST_MAP_READ)) {
#ifdef HAVE_GTK
        pixbuf = gdk_pixbuf_new_from_data (map.data,
            GDK_COLORSPACE_RGB, FALSE, 8, width, height,
            GST_ROUND_UP_4 (width * 3), NULL, NULL);

        /* save the pixbuf */
        gdk_pixbuf_save (pixbuf, "snapshot.png", "png", &error, NULL);
#endif
        gst_buffer_unmap (buffer, &map);
      }
      gst_sample_unref (sample);
    } else {
      g_print ("could not make snapshot\n");
    }

    /* cleanup and exit */
    gst_element_set_state (pipeline, GST_STATE_NULL);
    gst_object_unref (pipeline);

    exit (0);
}
```

19.3. Forcing a format

Sometimes you'll want to set a specific format, for example a video size and format or an audio bitsize and number of channels. You can do this by forcing a specific `GstCaps` on the pipeline, which is possible by using *filtered caps*. You can set a filtered caps on a link by using the "capsfilter" element in between the two elements, and specifying a `GstCaps` as "caps" property on this element. It will then only allow types matching that specified capability set for negotiation. See also Section 8.3.2.

19.3.1. Changing format in a PLAYING pipeline

It is also possible to dynamically change the format in a pipeline while PLAYING. This can simply be done by changing the caps property on a capsfilter. The capsfilter will send a RECONFIGURE event upstream that will make the upstream element attempt to renegotiate a new format and allocator. This only works if the upstream element is not using fixed caps on the source pad.

Below is an example of how you can change the caps of a pipeline while in the PLAYING state:

```
#include <stdlib.h>

#include <gst/gst.h>

#define MAX_ROUND 100

int
main (int argc, char **argv)
{
  GstElement *pipe, *filter;
  GstCaps *caps;
  gint width, height;
  gint xdir, ydir;
  gint round;
  GstMessage *message;

  gst_init (&argc, &argv);

  pipe = gst_parse_launch_full ("videotestsrc ! capsfilter name=filter ! "
            "ximagesink", NULL, GST_PARSE_FLAG_NONE, NULL);
  g_assert (pipe != NULL);

  filter = gst_bin_get_by_name (GST_BIN (pipe), "filter");
  g_assert (filter);

  width = 320;
  height = 240;
  xdir = ydir = -10;
```

```
for (round = 0; round < MAX_ROUND; round++) {
  gchar *capsstr;
  g_print ("resize to %dx%d (%d/%d)   \r", width, height, round, MAX_ROUND);

  /* we prefer our fixed width and height but allow other dimensions to pass
   * as well */
  capsstr = g_strdup_printf ("video/x-raw, width=(int)%d, height=(int)%d",
      width, height);

  caps = gst_caps_from_string (capsstr);
  g_free (capsstr);
  g_object_set (filter, "caps", caps, NULL);
  gst_caps_unref (caps);

  if (round == 0)
    gst_element_set_state (pipe, GST_STATE_PLAYING);

  width += xdir;
  if (width >= 320)
    xdir = -10;
  else if (width < 200)
    xdir = 10;

  height += ydir;
  if (height >= 240)
    ydir = -10;
  else if (height < 150)
    ydir = 10;

  message =
      gst_bus_poll (GST_ELEMENT_BUS (pipe), GST_MESSAGE_ERROR,
      50 * GST_MSECOND);
  if (message) {
    g_print ("got error            \n");

    gst_message_unref (message);
  }
}
g_print ("done                  \n");

gst_object_unref (filter);
gst_element_set_state (pipe, GST_STATE_NULL);
gst_object_unref (pipe);

return 0;
}
```

Note how we use `gst_bus_poll()` with a small timeout to get messages and also introduce a short sleep.

It is possible to set multiple caps for the capsfilter separated with a ;. The capsfilter will try to renegotiate to the first possible format from the list.

19.4. Dynamically changing the pipeline

In this section we talk about some techniques for dynamically modifying the pipeline. We are talking specifically about changing the pipeline while it is in the PLAYING state without interrupting the flow.

There are some important things to consider when building dynamic pipelines:

- When removing elements from the pipeline, make sure that there is no dataflow on unlinked pads because that will cause a fatal pipeline error. Always block source pads (in push mode) or sink pads (in pull mode) before unlinking pads. See also Section 19.4.1.

- When adding elements to a pipeline, make sure to put the element into the right state, usually the same state as the parent, before allowing dataflow the element. When an element is newly created, it is in the NULL state and will return an error when it receives data. See also Section 19.4.1.

- When adding elements to a pipeline, GStreamer will by default set the clock and base-time on the element to the current values of the pipeline. This means that the element will be able to construct the same pipeline running-time as the other elements in the pipeline. This means that sinks will synchronize buffers like the other sinks in the pipeline and that sources produce buffers with a running-time that matches the other sources.

- When unlinking elements from an upstream chain, always make sure to flush any queued data in the element by sending an EOS event down the element sink pad(s) and by waiting that the EOS leaves the elements (with an event probe).

  If you do not do this, you will lose the data which is buffered by the unlinked element. This can result in a simple frame loss (one or more video frames, several milliseconds of audio). However if you remove a muxer (and in some cases an encoder or similar elements) from the pipeline, you risk getting a corrupted file which could not be played properly, as some relevant metadata (header, seek/index tables, internal sync tags) will not be stored or updated properly.

  See also Section 19.4.1.

- A live source will produce buffers with a running-time of the current running-time in the pipeline.

  A pipeline without a live source produces buffers with a running-time starting from 0. Likewise, after a flushing seek, those pipelines reset the running-time back to 0.

  The running-time can be changed with `gst_pad_set_offset ()`. It is important to know the running-time of the elements in the pipeline in order to maintain synchronization.

- Adding elements might change the state of the pipeline. Adding a non-prerolled sink, for example, brings the pipeline back to the prerolling state. Removing a non-prerolled sink, for example, might change the pipeline to PAUSED and PLAYING state.

  Adding a live source cancels the preroll stage and put the pipeline to the playing state. Adding a live source or other live elements might also change the latency of a pipeline.

  Adding or removing elements to the pipeline might change the clock selection of the pipeline. If the newly added element provides a clock, it might be worth changing the clock in the pipeline to the new clock. If, on the other hand, the element that provides the clock for the pipeline is removed, a new clock has to be selected.

- Adding and removing elements might cause upstream or downstream elements to renegotiate caps and or allocators. You don't really need to do anything from the application, plugins largely adapt themself to the new pipeline topology in order to optimize their formats and allocation strategy.

  What is important is that when you add, remove or change elements in the pipeline, it is possible that the pipeline needs to negotiate a new format and this can fail. Usually you can fix this by inserting the right converter elements where needed. See also Section 19.4.1.

GStreamer offers support for doing about any dynamic pipeline modification but it requires you to know a bit of details before you can do this without causing pipeline errors. In the following sections we will demonstrate a couple of typical use-cases.

19.4.1. Changing elements in a pipeline

In the next example we look at the following chain of elements:

```
     - ----.         .----------.         .---- -
    element1 |       | element2 |        | element3
         src -> sink       src -> sink
     - ----'         '----------'         '---- -
```

We want to change element2 by element4 while the pipeline is in the PLAYING state. Let's say that element2 is a visualization and that you want to switch the visualization in the pipeline.

We can't just unlink element2's sinkpad from element1's source pad because that would leave element1's source pad unlinked and would cause a streaming error in the pipeline when data is pushed on the source pad. The technique is to block the dataflow from element1's source pad before we change element2 by element4 and then resume dataflow as shown in the following steps:

- Block element1's source pad with a blocking pad probe. When the pad is blocked, the probe callback will be called.

- Inside the block callback nothing is flowing between element1 and element2 and nothing will flow until unblocked.

- Unlink element1 and element2.

- Make sure data is flushed out of element2. Some elements might internally keep some data, you need to make sure not to lose data by forcing it out of element2. You can do this by pushing EOS into element2, like this:

  - Put an event probe on element2's source pad.

  - Send EOS to element2's sinkpad. This makes sure the all the data inside element2 is forced out.

  - Wait for the EOS event to appear on element2's source pad. When the EOS is received, drop it and remove the event probe.

- Unlink element2 and element3. You can now also remove element2 from the pipeline and set the state to NULL.

- Add element4 to the pipeline, if not already added. Link element4 and element3. Link element1 and element4.

- Make sure element4 is in the same state as the rest of the elements in the pipeline. It should be at least in the PAUSED state before it can receive buffers and events.

- Unblock element1's source pad probe. This will let new data into element4 and continue streaming.

The above algorithm works when the source pad is blocked, i.e. when there is dataflow in the pipeline. If there is no dataflow, there is also no point in changing the element (just yet) so this algorithm can be used in the PAUSED state as well.

Let show you how this works with an example. This example changes the video effect on a simple pipeline every second.


```
#include <gst/gst.h>

static gchar *opt_effects = NULL;

#define DEFAULT_EFFECTS "identity,exclusion,navigationtest," \
    "agingtv,videoflip,vertigotv,gaussianblur,shagadelictv,edgetv"

static GstPad *blockpad;
static GstElement *conv_before;
static GstElement *conv_after;
static GstElement *cur_effect;
static GstElement *pipeline;

static GQueue effects = G_QUEUE_INIT;
```

```
static GstPadProbeReturn
event_probe_cb (GstPad * pad, GstPadProbeInfo * info, gpointer user_data)
{
  GMainLoop *loop = user_data;
  GstElement *next;

  if (GST_EVENT_TYPE (GST_PAD_PROBE_INFO_DATA (info)) != GST_EVENT_EOS)
    return GST_PAD_PROBE_PASS;

  gst_pad_remove_probe (pad, GST_PAD_PROBE_INFO_ID (info));

  /* push current effect back into the queue */
  g_queue_push_tail (&effects, gst_object_ref (cur_effect));
  /* take next effect from the queue */
  next = g_queue_pop_head (&effects);
  if (next == NULL) {
    GST_DEBUG_OBJECT (pad, "no more effects");
    g_main_loop_quit (loop);
    return GST_PAD_PROBE_DROP;
  }

  g_print ("Switching from '%s' to '%s'..\n", GST_OBJECT_NAME (cur_effect),
      GST_OBJECT_NAME (next));

  gst_element_set_state (cur_effect, GST_STATE_NULL);

  /* remove unlinks automatically */
  GST_DEBUG_OBJECT (pipeline, "removing %" GST_PTR_FORMAT, cur_effect);
  gst_bin_remove (GST_BIN (pipeline), cur_effect);

  GST_DEBUG_OBJECT (pipeline, "adding   %" GST_PTR_FORMAT, next);
  gst_bin_add (GST_BIN (pipeline), next);

  GST_DEBUG_OBJECT (pipeline, "linking..");
  gst_element_link_many (conv_before, next, conv_after, NULL);

  gst_element_set_state (next, GST_STATE_PLAYING);

  cur_effect = next;
  GST_DEBUG_OBJECT (pipeline, "done");

  return GST_PAD_PROBE_DROP;
}

static GstPadProbeReturn
pad_probe_cb (GstPad * pad, GstPadProbeInfo * info, gpointer user_data)
{
  GstPad *srcpad, *sinkpad;

  GST_DEBUG_OBJECT (pad, "pad is blocked now");

  /* remove the probe first */
```

```
    gst_pad_remove_probe (pad, GST_PAD_PROBE_INFO_ID (info));

    /* install new probe for EOS */
    srcpad = gst_element_get_static_pad (cur_effect, "src");
    gst_pad_add_probe (srcpad, GST_PAD_PROBE_TYPE_BLOCK |
        GST_PAD_PROBE_TYPE_EVENT_DOWNSTREAM, event_probe_cb, user_data, NULL);
    gst_object_unref (srcpad);

    /* push EOS into the element, the probe will be fired when the
     * EOS leaves the effect and it has thus drained all of its data */
    sinkpad = gst_element_get_static_pad (cur_effect, "sink");
    gst_pad_send_event (sinkpad, gst_event_new_eos ());
    gst_object_unref (sinkpad);

    return GST_PAD_PROBE_OK;
}

static gboolean
timeout_cb (gpointer user_data)
{
  gst_pad_add_probe (blockpad, GST_PAD_PROBE_TYPE_BLOCK_DOWNSTREAM,
      pad_probe_cb, user_data, NULL);

  return TRUE;
}

static gboolean
bus_cb (GstBus * bus, GstMessage * msg, gpointer user_data)
{
  GMainLoop *loop = user_data;

  switch (GST_MESSAGE_TYPE (msg)) {
    case GST_MESSAGE_ERROR:{
      GError *err = NULL;
      gchar *dbg;

      gst_message_parse_error (msg, &err, &dbg);
      gst_object_default_error (msg->src, err, dbg);
      g_clear_error (&err);
      g_free (dbg);
      g_main_loop_quit (loop);
      break;
    }
    default:
      break;
  }
  return TRUE;
}

int
main (int argc, char **argv)
{
  GOptionEntry options[] = {
```

```
    {"effects", 'e', 0, G_OPTION_ARG_STRING, &opt_effects,
        "Effects to use (comma-separated list of element names)", NULL},
    {NULL}
};
GOptionContext *ctx;
GError *err = NULL;
GMainLoop *loop;
GstElement *src, *q1, *q2, *effect, *filter1, *filter2, *sink;
gchar **effect_names, **e;

ctx = g_option_context_new ("");
g_option_context_add_main_entries (ctx, options, NULL);
g_option_context_add_group (ctx, gst_init_get_option_group ());
if (!g_option_context_parse (ctx, &argc, &argv, &err)) {
  g_print ("Error initializing: %s\n", err->message);
  g_clear_error (&amp;err);
  g_option_context_free (ctx);
  return 1;
}
g_option_context_free (ctx);

if (opt_effects != NULL)
  effect_names = g_strsplit (opt_effects, ",", -1);
else
  effect_names = g_strsplit (DEFAULT_EFFECTS, ",", -1);

for (e = effect_names; e != NULL && *e != NULL; ++e) {
  GstElement *el;

  el = gst_element_factory_make (*e, NULL);
  if (el) {
    g_print ("Adding effect '%s'\n", *e);
    g_queue_push_tail (&effects, el);
  }
}

pipeline = gst_pipeline_new ("pipeline");

src = gst_element_factory_make ("videotestsrc", NULL);
g_object_set (src, "is-live", TRUE, NULL);

filter1 = gst_element_factory_make ("capsfilter", NULL);
gst_util_set_object_arg (G_OBJECT (filter1), "caps",
    "video/x-raw, width=320, height=240, "
    "format={ I420, YV12, YUY2, UYVY, AYUV, Y41B, Y42B, "
    "YVYU, Y444, v210, v216, NV12, NV21, UYVP, A420, YUV9, YVU9, IYU1 }");

q1 = gst_element_factory_make ("queue", NULL);

blockpad = gst_element_get_static_pad (q1, "src");

conv_before = gst_element_factory_make ("videoconvert", NULL);
```

```
    effect = g_queue_pop_head (&effects);
    cur_effect = effect;

    conv_after = gst_element_factory_make ("videoconvert", NULL);

    q2 = gst_element_factory_make ("queue", NULL);

    filter2 = gst_element_factory_make ("capsfilter", NULL);
    gst_util_set_object_arg (G_OBJECT (filter2), "caps",
        "video/x-raw, width=320, height=240, "
        "format={ RGBx, BGRx, xRGB, xBGR, RGBA, BGRA, ARGB, ABGR, RGB, BGR }");

    sink = gst_element_factory_make ("ximagesink", NULL);

    gst_bin_add_many (GST_BIN (pipeline), src, filter1, q1, conv_before, effect,
        conv_after, q2, sink, NULL);

    gst_element_link_many (src, filter1, q1, conv_before, effect, conv_after,
        q2, sink, NULL);

    gst_element_set_state (pipeline, GST_STATE_PLAYING);

    loop = g_main_loop_new (NULL, FALSE);

    gst_bus_add_watch (GST_ELEMENT_BUS (pipeline), bus_cb, loop);

    g_timeout_add_seconds (1, timeout_cb, loop);

    g_main_loop_run (loop);

    gst_element_set_state (pipeline, GST_STATE_NULL);
    gst_object_unref (pipeline);

    return 0;
}
```

Note how we added videoconvert elements before and after the effect. This is needed because some elements might operate in different colorspaces than other elements. By inserting the conversion elements you ensure that the right format can be negotiated at any time.

IV. Higher-level interfaces for GStreamer applications

In the previous two parts, you have learned many of the internals and their corresponding low-level interfaces into GStreamer application programming. Many people will, however, not need so much control (and as much code), but will prefer to use a standard playback interface that does most of the difficult internals for them. In this chapter, we will introduce you into the concept of autopluggers, playback managing elements and other such things. Those higher-level interfaces are intended to simplify GStreamer-based application programming. They do, however, also reduce the flexibility. It is up to the application developer to choose which interface he will want to use.

Chapter 20. Playback Components

GStreamer includes several higher-level components to simplify an application developer's life. All of the components discussed here (for now) are targetted at media playback. The idea of each of these components is to integrate as closely as possible with a GStreamer pipeline, but to hide the complexity of media type detection and several other rather complex topics that have been discussed in Part III in *GStreamer Application Development Manual (1.8.3)*.

We currently recommend people to use either playbin (see Section 20.1) or decodebin (see Section 20.2), depending on their needs. Playbin is the recommended solution for everything related to simple playback of media that should just work. Decodebin is a more flexible autoplugger that could be used to add more advanced features, such as playlist support, crossfading of audio tracks and so on. Its programming interface is more low-level than that of playbin, though.

20.1. Playbin

Playbin is an element that can be created using the standard GStreamer API (e.g. `gst_element_factory_make ()`). The factory is conveniently called "playbin". By being a `GstPipeline` (and thus a `GstElement`), playbin automatically supports all of the features of this class, including error handling, tag support, state handling, getting stream positions, seeking, and so on.

Setting up a playbin pipeline is as simple as creating an instance of the playbin element, setting a file location using the "uri" property on playbin, and then setting the element to the `GST_STATE_PLAYING` state (the location has to be a valid URI, so "<protocol>://<location>", e.g. file:///tmp/my.ogg or http://www.example.org/stream.ogg). Internally, playbin will set up a pipeline to playback the media location.

```
#include <gst/gst.h>

[.. my_bus_callback goes here ..]

gint
main (gint    argc,
      gchar *argv[])
{
  GMainLoop *loop;
  GstElement *play;
  GstBus *bus;

  /* init GStreamer */
  gst_init (&argc, &argv);
  loop = g_main_loop_new (NULL, FALSE);

  /* make sure we have a URI */
  if (argc != 2) {
```

```
    g_print ("Usage: %s <URI>\n", argv[0]);
    return -1;
  }

  /* set up */
  play = gst_element_factory_make ("playbin", "play");
  g_object_set (G_OBJECT (play), "uri", argv[1], NULL);

  bus = gst_pipeline_get_bus (GST_PIPELINE (play));
  gst_bus_add_watch (bus, my_bus_callback, loop);
  gst_object_unref (bus);

  gst_element_set_state (play, GST_STATE_PLAYING);

  /* now run */
  g_main_loop_run (loop);

  /* also clean up */
  gst_element_set_state (play, GST_STATE_NULL);
  gst_object_unref (GST_OBJECT (play));

  return 0;
}
```

Playbin has several features that have been discussed previously:

- Settable video and audio output (using the "video-sink" and "audio-sink" properties).

- Mostly controllable and trackable as a `GstElement`, including error handling, eos handling, tag handling, state handling (through the `GstBus`), media position handling and seeking.

- Buffers network-sources, with buffer fullness notifications being passed through the `GstBus`.

- Supports visualizations for audio-only media.

- Supports subtitles, both in the media as well as from separate files. For separate subtitle files, use the "suburi" property.

- Supports stream selection and disabling. If your media has multiple audio or subtitle tracks, you can dynamically choose which one to play back, or decide to turn it off altogether (which is especially useful to turn off subtitles). For each of those, use the "current-text" and other related properties.

For convenience, it is possible to test "playbin" on the commandline, using the command "gst-launch-1.0 playbin uri=file:///path/to/file".

20.2. Decodebin

Decodebin is the actual autoplugger backend of playbin, which was discussed in the previous section. Decodebin will, in short, accept input from a source that is linked to its sinkpad and will try to detect the media type contained in the stream, and set up decoder routines for each of those. It will automatically select decoders. For each decoded stream, it will emit the "pad-added" signal, to let the client know about the newly found decoded stream. For unknown streams (which might be the whole stream), it will emit the "unknown-type" signal. The application is then responsible for reporting the error to the user.

```
#include <gst/gst.h>


[.. my_bus_callback goes here ..]



GstElement *pipeline, *audio;

static void
cb_newpad (GstElement *decodebin,
    GstPad     *pad,
    gpointer    data)
{
  GstCaps *caps;
  GstStructure *str;
  GstPad *audiopad;

  /* only link once */
  audiopad = gst_element_get_static_pad (audio, "sink");
  if (GST_PAD_IS_LINKED (audiopad)) {
    g_object_unref (audiopad);
    return;
  }

  /* check media type */
  caps = gst_pad_query_caps (pad, NULL);
  str = gst_caps_get_structure (caps, 0);
  if (!g_strrstr (gst_structure_get_name (str), "audio")) {
    gst_caps_unref (caps);
    gst_object_unref (audiopad);
    return;
  }
  gst_caps_unref (caps);

  /* link'n'play */
  gst_pad_link (pad, audiopad);

  g_object_unref (audiopad);
}

gint
main (gint   argc,
      gchar *argv[])
{
  GMainLoop *loop;
  GstElement *src, *dec, *conv, *sink;
```

```
    GstPad *audiopad;
    GstBus *bus;

    /* init GStreamer */
    gst_init (&argc, &argv);
    loop = g_main_loop_new (NULL, FALSE);

    /* make sure we have input */
    if (argc != 2) {
      g_print ("Usage: %s <filename>\n", argv[0]);
      return -1;
    }

    /* setup */
    pipeline = gst_pipeline_new ("pipeline");

    bus = gst_pipeline_get_bus (GST_PIPELINE (pipeline));
    gst_bus_add_watch (bus, my_bus_callback, loop);
    gst_object_unref (bus);

    src = gst_element_factory_make ("filesrc", "source");
    g_object_set (G_OBJECT (src), "location", argv[1], NULL);
    dec = gst_element_factory_make ("decodebin", "decoder");
    g_signal_connect (dec, "pad-added", G_CALLBACK (cb_newpad), NULL);
    gst_bin_add_many (GST_BIN (pipeline), src, dec, NULL);
    gst_element_link (src, dec);

    /* create audio output */
    audio = gst_bin_new ("audiobin");
    conv = gst_element_factory_make ("audioconvert", "aconv");
    audiopad = gst_element_get_static_pad (conv, "sink");
    sink = gst_element_factory_make ("alsasink", "sink");
    gst_bin_add_many (GST_BIN (audio), conv, sink, NULL);
    gst_element_link (conv, sink);
    gst_element_add_pad (audio,
        gst_ghost_pad_new ("sink", audiopad));
    gst_object_unref (audiopad);
    gst_bin_add (GST_BIN (pipeline), audio);

    /* run */
    gst_element_set_state (pipeline, GST_STATE_PLAYING);
    g_main_loop_run (loop);

    /* cleanup */
    gst_element_set_state (pipeline, GST_STATE_NULL);
    gst_object_unref (GST_OBJECT (pipeline));

    return 0;
}
```

Decodebin, similar to playbin, supports the following features:

- Can decode an unlimited number of contained streams to decoded output pads.
- Is handled as a `GstElement` in all ways, including tag or error forwarding and state handling.

Although decodebin is a good autoplugger, there's a whole lot of things that it does not do and is not intended to do:

- Taking care of input streams with a known media type (e.g. a DVD, an audio-CD or such).
- Selection of streams (e.g. which audio track to play in case of multi-language media streams).
- Overlaying subtitles over a decoded video stream.

Decodebin can be easily tested on the commandline, e.g. by using the command **gst-launch-1.0 filesrc location=file.ogg ! decodebin ! audioconvert ! audioresample ! autoaudiosink**.

20.3. URIDecodebin

The uridecodebin element is very similar to decodebin, only that it automatically plugs a source plugin based on the protocol of the URI given.

Uridecodebin will also automatically insert buffering elements when the uri is a slow network source. The buffering element will post BUFFERING messages that the application needs to handle as explained in Chapter 15. The following properties can be used to configure the buffering method:

- The buffer-size property allows you to configure a maximum size in bytes for the buffer element.
- The buffer-duration property allows you to configure a maximum size in time for the buffer element. The time will be estimated based on the bitrate of the network.
- With the download property you can enable the download buffering method as described in Section 15.2. Setting this option to TRUE will only enable download buffering for selected formats such as quicktime, flash video, avi and webm.
- You can also enable buffering on the parsed/demuxed data with the use-buffering property. This is interesting to enable buffering on slower random access media such as a network file server.

URIDecodebin can be easily tested on the commandline, e.g. by using the command **gst-launch-1.0 uridecodebin uri=file:///file.ogg ! ! audioconvert ! audioresample ! autoaudiosink**.

20.4. Playsink

The playsink element is a powerful sink element. It has request pads for raw decoded audio, video and text and it will configure itself to play the media streams. It has the following features:

- It exposes GstStreamVolume, GstVideoOverlay, GstNavigation and GstColorBalance interfaces and automatically plugs software elements to implement the interfaces when needed.

- It will automatically plug conversion elements.

- Can optionally render visualizations when there is no video input.

- Configurable sink elements.

- Configurable audio/video sync offset to fine-tune synchronization in badly muxed files.

- Support for taking a snapshot of the last video frame.

Below is an example of how you can use playsink. We use a uridecodebin element to decode into raw audio and video streams which we then link to the playsink request pads. We only link the first audio and video pads, you could use an input-selector to link all pads.

```
#include <gst/gst.h>


[.. my_bus_callback goes here ..]




GstElement *pipeline, *sink;

static void
cb_pad_added (GstElement *dec,
      GstPad       *pad,
      gpointer     data)
{
  GstCaps *caps;
  GstStructure *str;
  const gchar *name;
  GstPadTemplate *templ;
  GstElementClass *klass;

  /* check media type */
  caps = gst_pad_query_caps (pad, NULL);
  str = gst_caps_get_structure (caps, 0);
  name = gst_structure_get_name (str);

  klass = GST_ELEMENT_GET_CLASS (sink);

  if (g_str_has_prefix (name, "audio")) {
    templ = gst_element_class_get_pad_template (klass, "audio_sink");
  } else if (g_str_has_prefix (name, "video")) {
    templ = gst_element_class_get_pad_template (klass, "video_sink");
  } else if (g_str_has_prefix (name, "text")) {
    templ = gst_element_class_get_pad_template (klass, "text_sink");
```

```
    } else {
      templ = NULL;
    }

    if (templ) {
      GstPad *sinkpad;

      sinkpad = gst_element_request_pad (sink, templ, NULL, NULL);

      if (!gst_pad_is_linked (sinkpad))
        gst_pad_link (pad, sinkpad);

      gst_object_unref (sinkpad);
    }
}

gint
main (gint   argc,
      gchar *argv[])
{
  GMainLoop *loop;
  GstElement *dec;
  GstBus *bus;

  /* init GStreamer */
  gst_init (&argc, &argv);
  loop = g_main_loop_new (NULL, FALSE);

  /* make sure we have input */
  if (argc != 2) {
    g_print ("Usage: %s <uri>\n", argv[0]);
    return -1;
  }

  /* setup */
  pipeline = gst_pipeline_new ("pipeline");

  bus = gst_pipeline_get_bus (GST_PIPELINE (pipeline));
  gst_bus_add_watch (bus, my_bus_callback, loop);
  gst_object_unref (bus);

  dec = gst_element_factory_make ("uridecodebin", "source");
  g_object_set (G_OBJECT (dec), "uri", argv[1], NULL);
  g_signal_connect (dec, "pad-added", G_CALLBACK (cb_pad_added), NULL);

  /* create audio output */
  sink = gst_element_factory_make ("playsink", "sink");
  gst_util_set_object_arg (G_OBJECT (sink), "flags",
      "soft-colorbalance+soft-volume+vis+text+audio+video");
  gst_bin_add_many (GST_BIN (pipeline), dec, sink, NULL);

  /* run */
  gst_element_set_state (pipeline, GST_STATE_PLAYING);
```

```
    g_main_loop_run (loop);

    /* cleanup */
    gst_element_set_state (pipeline, GST_STATE_NULL);
    gst_object_unref (GST_OBJECT (pipeline));

    return 0;
}
```

This example will show audio and video depending on what you give it. Try this example on an audio file and you will see that it shows visualizations. You can change the visualization at runtime by changing the vis-plugin property.

V. Appendices

By now, you've learned all about the internals of GStreamer and application programming using the GStreamer framework. This part will go into some random bits that are useful to know if you're going to use GStreamer for serious application programming. It will touch upon things related to integration with popular desktop environments that we run on (GNOME, KDE, OS X, Windows), it will shortly explain how applications included with GStreamer can help making your life easier, and some information on debugging.

In addition, we also provide a porting guide which will explain easily how to port GStreamer-0.10 applications to GStreamer-1.0.

Chapter 21. Programs

21.1. gst-launch

This is a tool that will construct pipelines based on a command-line syntax.

A simple commandline looks like:

```
gst-launch filesrc location=hello.mp3 ! mad ! audioresample ! osssink
```

A more complex pipeline looks like:

```
gst-launch filesrc location=redpill.vob ! dvddemux name=demux \
 demux.audio_00 ! queue ! a52dec ! audioconvert ! audioresample ! osssink \
 demux.video_00 ! queue ! mpeg2dec ! videoconvert ! xvimagesink
```

You can also use the parser in you own code. GStreamer provides a function gst_parse_launch () that you can use to construct a pipeline. The following program lets you create an MP3 pipeline using the gst_parse_launch () function:

```
#include <gst/gst.h>

int
main (int argc, char *argv[])
{
  GstElement *pipeline;
  GstElement *filesrc;
  GstMessage *msg;
  GstBus *bus;
  GError *error = NULL;

  gst_init (&argc, &argv);

  if (argc != 2) {
    g_print ("usage: %s <filename>\n", argv[0]);
    return -1;
  }

  pipeline = gst_parse_launch ("filesrc name=my_filesrc ! mad ! osssink", &error);
  if (!pipeline) {
    g_print ("Parse error: %s\n", error->message);
    exit (1);
```

```
    }

    filesrc = gst_bin_get_by_name (GST_BIN (pipeline), "my_filesrc");
    g_object_set (filesrc, "location", argv[1], NULL);
    g_object_unref (filesrc);

    gst_element_set_state (pipeline, GST_STATE_PLAYING);

    bus = gst_element_get_bus (pipeline);

    /* wait until we either get an EOS or an ERROR message. Note that in a real
     * program you would probably not use gst_bus_poll(), but rather set up an
     * async signal watch on the bus and run a main loop and connect to the
     * bus's signals to catch certain messages or all messages */
    msg = gst_bus_poll (bus, GST_MESSAGE_EOS | GST_MESSAGE_ERROR, -1);

    switch (GST_MESSAGE_TYPE (msg)) {
      case GST_MESSAGE_EOS: {
        g_print ("EOS\n");
        break;
      }
      case GST_MESSAGE_ERROR: {
        GError *err = NULL; /* error to show to users                 */
        gchar *dbg = NULL;  /* additional debug string for developers */

        gst_message_parse_error (msg, &err, &dbg);
        if (err) {
          g_printerr ("ERROR: %s\n", err->message);
          g_error_free (err);
        }
        if (dbg) {
          g_printerr ("[Debug details: %s]\n", dbg);
          g_free (dbg);
        }
      }
      default:
        g_printerr ("Unexpected message of type %d", GST_MESSAGE_TYPE (msg));
        break;
    }
    gst_message_unref (msg);

    gst_element_set_state (pipeline, GST_STATE_NULL);
    gst_object_unref (pipeline);
    gst_object_unref (bus);

    return 0;
}
```

Note how we can retrieve the filesrc element from the constructed bin using the element name.

21.1.1. Grammar Reference

The **gst-launch** syntax is processed by a flex/bison parser. This section is intended to provide a full specification of the grammar; any deviations from this specification is considered a bug.

21.1.1.1. Elements

```
... mad ...
```

A bare identifier (a string beginning with a letter and containing only letters, numbers, dashes, underscores, percent signs, or colons) will create an element from a given element factory. In this example, an instance of the "mad" MP3 decoding plugin will be created.

21.1.1.2. Links

```
... !sink ...
```

An exclamation point, optionally having a qualified pad name (an the name of the pad, optionally preceded by the name of the element) on both sides, will link two pads. If the source pad is not specified, a source pad from the immediately preceding element will be automatically chosen. If the sink pad is not specified, a sink pad from the next element to be constructed will be chosen. An attempt will be made to find compatible pads. Pad names may be preceded by an element name, as in `my_element_name.sink_pad`.

21.1.1.3. Properties

```
... location="http://gstreamer.net" ...
```

The name of a property, optionally qualified with an element name, and a value, separated by an equals sign, will set a property on an element. If the element is not specified, the previous element is assumed. Strings can optionally be enclosed in quotation marks. Characters in strings may be escaped with the backtick (\). If the right-hand side is all digits, it is considered to be an integer. If it is all digits and a decimal point, it is a double. If it is "true", "false", "TRUE", or "FALSE" it is considered to be boolean. Otherwise, it is parsed as a string. The type of the property is determined later on in the parsing, and the value is converted to the target type. This conversion is not guaranteed to work, it relies on the g_value_convert routines. No error message will be displayed on an invalid conversion, due to limitations in the value convert API.

21.1.1.4. Bins, Threads, and Pipelines

```
( ... )
```

A pipeline description between parentheses is placed into a bin. The open paren may be preceded by a type name, as in `jackbin. ( ... )` to make a bin of a specified type. Square brackets make pipelines, and curly braces make threads. The default toplevel bin type is a pipeline, although putting the whole description within parentheses or braces can override this default.

21.2. gst-inspect

This is a tool to query a plugin or an element about its properties.

To query the information about the element mad, you would specify:

```
gst-inspect mad
```

Below is the output of a query for the osssink element:

```
Factory Details:
  Rank:           secondary (128)
  Long-name:          Audio Sink (OSS)
  Klass:              Sink/Audio
  Description:        Output to a sound card via OSS
  Author:             Erik Walthinsen <omega@cse.ogi.edu>, Wim Taymans <wim.taymans@che

Plugin Details:
  Name:               ossaudio
  Description:        OSS (Open Sound System) support for GStreamer
  Filename:           /home/wim/gst/head/gst-plugins-good/sys/oss/.libs/libgstossaudio.
  Version:            1.0.0.1
  License:            LGPL
  Source module:      gst-plugins-good
  Source release date: 2012-09-25 12:52 (UTC)
  Binary package:     GStreamer Good Plug-ins git
  Origin URL:         Unknown package origin

GObject
 +----GInitiallyUnowned
       +----GstObject
             +----GstElement
                   +----GstBaseSink
                         +----GstAudioBaseSink
                               +----GstAudioSink
                                     +----GstOssSink
```

```
Pad Templates:
  SINK template: 'sink'
    Availability: Always
    Capabilities:
      audio/x-raw
                  format: { S16LE, U16LE, S8, U8 }
                  layout: interleaved
                    rate: [ 1, 2147483647 ]
                channels: 1
      audio/x-raw
                  format: { S16LE, U16LE, S8, U8 }
                  layout: interleaved
                    rate: [ 1, 2147483647 ]
                channels: 2
            channel-mask: 0x0000000000000003


Element Flags:
  no flags set

Element Implementation:
  Has change_state() function: gst_audio_base_sink_change_state

Clocking Interaction:
  element is supposed to provide a clock but returned NULL

Element has no indexing capabilities.
Element has no URI handling capabilities.

Pads:
  SINK: 'sink'
    Implementation:
      Has chainfunc(): gst_base_sink_chain
      Has custom eventfunc(): gst_base_sink_event
      Has custom queryfunc(): gst_base_sink_sink_query
      Has custom iterintlinkfunc(): gst_pad_iterate_internal_links_default
    Pad Template: 'sink'

Element Properties:
  name                : The name of the object
                        flags: readable, writable
                        String. Default: "osssink0"
  parent              : The parent of the object
                        flags: readable, writable
                        Object of type "GstObject"
  sync                : Sync on the clock
                        flags: readable, writable
                        Boolean. Default: true
  max-lateness        : Maximum number of nanoseconds that a buffer can be late before it
                        flags: readable, writable
                        Integer64. Range: -1 - 9223372036854775807 Default: -1
  qos                 : Generate Quality-of-Service events upstream
                        flags: readable, writable
```

```
                              Boolean. Default: false
  async               : Go asynchronously to PAUSED
                              flags: readable, writable
                              Boolean. Default: true
  ts-offset           : Timestamp offset in nanoseconds
                              flags: readable, writable
                              Integer64. Range: -9223372036854775808 - 9223372036854775807 Def
  enable-last-sample  : Enable the last-sample property
                              flags: readable, writable
                              Boolean. Default: false
  last-sample         : The last sample received in the sink
                              flags: readable
                              Boxed pointer of type "GstSample"
  blocksize           : Size in bytes to pull per buffer (0 = default)
                              flags: readable, writable
                              Unsigned Integer. Range: 0 - 4294967295 Default: 4096
  render-delay        : Additional render delay of the sink in nanoseconds
                              flags: readable, writable
                              Unsigned Integer64. Range: 0 - 18446744073709551615 Default: 0
  throttle-time       : The time to keep between rendered buffers
                              flags: readable, writable
                              Unsigned Integer64. Range: 0 - 18446744073709551615 Default: 0
  buffer-time         : Size of audio buffer in microseconds, this is the minimum latenc
                              flags: readable, writable
                              Integer64. Range: 1 - 9223372036854775807 Default: 200000
  latency-time        : The minimum amount of data to write in each iteration in microse
                              flags: readable, writable
                              Integer64. Range: 1 - 9223372036854775807 Default: 10000
  provide-clock       : Provide a clock to be used as the global pipeline clock
                              flags: readable, writable
                              Boolean. Default: true
  slave-method        : Algorithm to use to match the rate of the masterclock
                              flags: readable, writable
                              Enum "GstAudioBaseSinkSlaveMethod" Default: 1, "skew"
                                 (0): resample         - GST_AUDIO_BASE_SINK_SLAVE_RESAMPLE
                                 (1): skew             - GST_AUDIO_BASE_SINK_SLAVE_SKEW
                                 (2): none             - GST_AUDIO_BASE_SINK_SLAVE_NONE
  can-activate-pull   : Allow pull-based scheduling
                              flags: readable, writable
                              Boolean. Default: false
  alignment-threshold : Timestamp alignment threshold in nanoseconds
                              flags: readable, writable
                              Unsigned Integer64. Range: 1 - 18446744073709551614 Default: 400
  drift-tolerance     : Tolerance for clock drift in microseconds
                              flags: readable, writable
                              Integer64. Range: 1 - 9223372036854775807 Default: 40000
  discont-wait        : Window of time in nanoseconds to wait before creating a disconti
                              flags: readable, writable
                              Unsigned Integer64. Range: 0 - 18446744073709551614 Default: 100
  device              : OSS device (usually /dev/dspN)
                              flags: readable, writable
                              String. Default: "/dev/dsp"
```

To query the information about a plugin, you would do:

```
gst-inspect gstelements
```

Chapter 22. Compiling

This section talks about the different things you can do when building and shipping your applications and plugins.

22.1. Embedding static elements in your application

The Plugin Writer's Guide (http://gstreamer.freedesktop.org/data/doc/gstreamer/head/pwg/html/index.html) describes in great detail how to write elements for the GStreamer framework. In this section, we will solely discuss how to embed such elements statically in your application. This can be useful for application-specific elements that have no use elsewhere in GStreamer.

Dynamically loaded plugins contain a structure that's defined using GST_PLUGIN_DEFINE (). This structure is loaded when the plugin is loaded by the GStreamer core. The structure contains an initialization function (usually called plugin_init) that will be called right after that. It's purpose is to register the elements provided by the plugin with the GStreamer framework. If you want to embed elements directly in your application, the only thing you need to do is to replace GST_PLUGIN_DEFINE () with a call to gst_plugin_register_static (). As soon as you call gst_plugin_register_static (), the elements will from then on be available like any other element, without them having to be dynamically loadable libraries. In the example below, you would be able to call gst_element_factory_make ("my-element-name", "some-name") to create an instance of the element.

```
/*
 * Here, you would write the actual plugin code.
 */

[..]

static gboolean
register_elements (GstPlugin *plugin)
{
  return gst_element_register (plugin, "my-element-name",
      GST_RANK_NONE, MY_PLUGIN_TYPE);
}

static
my_code_init (void)
{
  ...

  gst_plugin_register_static (
    GST_VERSION_MAJOR,
    GST_VERSION_MINOR,
```

```
      "my-private-plugins",
      "Private elements of my application",
      register_elements,
      VERSION,
      "LGPL",
      "my-application-source",
      "my-application",
      "http://www.my-application.net/")

    ...
}
```

Chapter 23. Things to check when writing an application

This chapter contains a fairly random selection of things that can be useful to keep in mind when writing GStreamer-based applications. It's up to you how much you're going to use the information provided here. We will shortly discuss how to debug pipeline problems using GStreamer applications. Also, we will touch upon how to acquire knowledge about plugins and elements and how to test simple pipelines before building applications around them.

23.1. Good programming habits

- Always add a `GstBus` handler to your pipeline. Always report errors in your application, and try to do something with warnings and information messages, too.

- Always check return values of GStreamer functions. Especially, check return values of `gst_element_link ()` and `gst_element_set_state ()`.

- Dereference return values of all functions returning a non-base type, such as `gst_element_get_pad ()`. Also, always free non-const string returns, such as `gst_object_get_name ()`.

- Always use your pipeline object to keep track of the current state of your pipeline. Don't keep private variables in your application. Also, don't update your user interface if a user presses the "play" button. Instead, listen for the "state-changed" message on the `GstBus` and only update the user interface whenever this message is received.

- Report all bugs that you find in GStreamer bugzilla at http://bugzilla.gnome.org/ (http://bugzilla.gnome.org).

23.2. Debugging

Applications can make use of the extensive GStreamer debugging system to debug pipeline problems. Elements will write output to this system to log what they're doing. It's not used for error reporting, but it is very useful for tracking what an element is doing exactly, which can come in handy when debugging application issues (such as failing seeks, out-of-sync media, etc.).

Most GStreamer-based applications accept the commandline option `--gst-debug=LIST` and related family members. The list consists of a comma-separated list of category/level pairs, which can set the debugging level for a specific debugging category. For example, `--gst-debug=oggdemux:5` would turn on debugging for the Ogg demuxer element. You can use wildcards as well. A debugging level of 0 will turn off all debugging, and a level of 9 will turn on all debugging. Intermediate values only turn on some debugging (based on message severity; 2, for example, will only display errors and warnings). Here's a list of all available options:

- `--gst-debug-help` will print available debug categories and exit.

- `--gst-debug-level=LEVEL` will set the default debug level (which can range from 0 (no output) to 9 (everything)).

- `--gst-debug=LIST` takes a comma-separated list of category_name:level pairs to set specific levels for the individual categories. Example: `GST_AUTOPLUG:5,avidemux:3`. Alternatively, you can also set the `GST_DEBUG` environment variable, which has the same effect.

- `--gst-debug-no-color` will disable color debugging. You can also set the GST_DEBUG_NO_COLOR environment variable to 1 if you want to disable colored debug output permanently. Note that if you are disabling color purely to avoid messing up your pager output, try using **less -R**.

- `--gst-debug-color-mode=MODE` will change debug log coloring mode. *MODE* can be one of the following: `on`, `off`, `auto`, `disable`, `unix`. You can also set the GST_DEBUG_COLOR_MODE environment variable if you want to change colored debug output permanently. Note that if you are disabling color purely to avoid messing up your pager output, try using **less -R**.

- `--gst-debug-disable` disables debugging altogether.

- `--gst-plugin-spew` enables printout of errors while loading GStreamer plugins.

23.3. Conversion plugins

GStreamer contains a bunch of conversion plugins that most applications will find useful. Specifically, those are videoscalers (videoscale), colorspace convertors (videoconvert), audio format convertors and channel resamplers (audioconvert) and audio samplerate convertors (audioresample). Those convertors don't do anything when not required, they will act in passthrough mode. They will activate when the hardware doesn't support a specific request, though. All applications are recommended to use those elements.

23.4. Utility applications provided with GStreamer

GStreamer comes with a default set of command-line utilities that can help in application development. We will discuss only **gst-launch** and **gst-inspect** here.

23.4.1. gst-launch

gst-launch is a simple script-like commandline application that can be used to test pipelines. For example, the command **gst-launch audiotestsrc ! audioconvert ! audio/x-raw,channels=2 ! alsasink** will run a pipeline which generates a sine-wave audio stream and plays it to your ALSA audio card. **gst-launch** also allows the use of threads (will be used automatically as required or as queue elements are inserted in the pipeline) and bins (using brackets, so "(" and ")"). You can use dots to imply padnames on elements, or even omit the padname to automatically select a pad. Using all this, the pipeline **gst-launch filesrc location=file.ogg ! oggdemux name=d d. ! queue ! theoradec ! videoconvert ! xvimagesink d. ! queue ! vorbisdec ! audioconvert ! audioresample ! alsasink** will play an Ogg file containing a Theora video-stream and a Vorbis audio-stream. You can also use autopluggers such as decodebin on the commandline. See the manual page of **gst-launch** for more information.

23.4.2. gst-inspect

gst-inspect can be used to inspect all properties, signals, dynamic parameters and the object hierarchy of an element. This can be very useful to see which GObject properties or which signals (and using what arguments) an element supports. Run **gst-inspect fakesrc** to get an idea of what it does. See the manual page of **gst-inspect** for more information.

Chapter 24. Porting 0.8 applications to 0.10

This section of the appendix will discuss shortly what changes to applications will be needed to quickly and conveniently port most applications from GStreamer-0.8 to GStreamer-0.10, with references to the relevant sections in this Application Development Manual where needed. With this list, it should be possible to port simple applications to GStreamer-0.10 in less than a day.

24.1. List of changes

- Most functions returning an object or an object property have been changed to return its own reference rather than a constant reference of the one owned by the object itself. The reason for this change is primarily thread safety. This means, effectively, that return values of functions such as `gst_element_get_pad ()`, `gst_pad_get_name ()` and many more like these have to be free'ed or unreferenced after use. Check the API references of each function to know for sure whether return values should be free'ed or not. It is important that all objects derived from GstObject are ref'ed/unref'ed using gst_object_ref() and gst_object_unref() respectively (instead of g_object_ref/unref).

- Applications should no longer use signal handlers to be notified of errors, end-of-stream and other similar pipeline events. Instead, they should use the `GstBus`, which has been discussed in Chapter 7. The bus will take care that the messages will be delivered in the context of a main loop, which is almost certainly the application's main thread. The big advantage of this is that applications no longer need to be thread-aware; they don't need to use `g_idle_add ()` in the signal handler and do the actual real work in the idle-callback. GStreamer now does all that internally.

- Related to this, `gst_bin_iterate ()` has been removed. Pipelines will iterate in their own thread, and applications can simply run a `GMainLoop` (or call the mainloop of their UI toolkit, such as `gtk_main ()`).

- State changes can be delayed (ASYNC). Due to the new fully threaded nature of GStreamer-0.10, state changes are not always immediate, in particular changes including the transition from READY to PAUSED state. This means two things in the context of porting applications: first of all, it is no longer always possible to do `gst_element_set_state ()` and check for a return value of GST_STATE_CHANGE_SUCCESS, as the state change might be delayed (ASYNC) and the result will not be known until later. You should still check for GST_STATE_CHANGE_FAILURE right away, it is just no longer possible to assume that everything that is not SUCCESS means failure. Secondly, state changes might not be immediate, so your code needs to take that into account. You can wait for a state change to complete if you use GST_CLOCK_TIME_NONE as timeout interval with `gst_element_get_state ()`.

- In 0.8, events and queries had to manually be sent to sinks in pipelines (unless you were using playbin). This is no longer the case in 0.10. In 0.10, queries and events can be sent to toplevel pipelines, and the pipeline will do the dispatching internally for you. This means less bookkeeping in your application. For a short code example, see Chapter 11. Related, seeking is now threadsafe, and your video output will show the new video position's frame while seeking, providing a better user experience.

- The `GstThread` object has been removed. Applications can now simply put elements in a pipeline with optionally some "queue" elements in between for buffering, and GStreamer will take care of creating threads internally. It is still possible to have parts of a pipeline run in different threads than others, by using the "queue" element. See Chapter 17 for details.

- Filtered caps -> capsfilter element (the pipeline syntax for gst-launch has not changed though).

- libgstgconf-0.10.la does not exist. Use the "gconfvideosink" and "gconfaudiosink" elements instead, which will do live-updates and require no library linking.

- The "new-pad" and "state-change" signals on `GstElement` were renamed to "pad-added" and "state-changed".

- `gst_init_get_popt_table ()` has been removed in favour of the new GOption command line option API that was added to GLib 2.6. `gst_init_get_option_group ()` is the new GOption-based equivalent to `gst_init_get_ptop_table ()`.

Chapter 25. Porting 0.10 applications to 1.0

This section outlines some of the changes necessary to port applications from GStreamer-0.10 to GStreamer-1.0. For a comprehensive and up-to-date list, see the separate Porting to 1.0 (http://cgit.freedesktop.org/gstreamer/gstreamer/plain/docs/random/porting-to-1.0.txt) document.

It should be possible to port simple applications to GStreamer-1.0 in less than a day.

25.1. List of changes

- All deprecated methods were removed. Recompile against 0.10 with GST_DISABLE_DEPRECATED defined (such as by adding -DGST_DISABLE_DEPRECATED to the compiler flags) and fix issues before attempting to port to 1.0.

- "playbin2" has been renamed to "playbin", with similar API

- "decodebin2" has been renamed to "decodebin", with similar API. Note that there is no longer a "new-decoded-pad" signal, just use GstElement's "pad-added" signal instead (but don't forget to remove the 'gboolean last' argument from your old signal callback functino signature).

- the names of some "formatted" pad templates has been changed from e.g. "src%d" to "src%u" or "src_%u" or similar, since we don't want to see negative numbers in pad names. This mostly affects applications that create request pads from elements.

- some elements that used to have a single dynamic source pad have a source pad now. Example: wavparse, id3demux, iceydemux, apedemux. (This does not affect applications using decodebin or playbin).

- playbin now proxies the GstVideoOverlay (former GstXOverlay) interface, so most applications can just remove the sync bus handler where they would set the window ID, and instead just set the window ID on playbin from the application thread before starting playback.

  playbin also proxies the GstColorBalance and GstNavigation interfaces, so applications that use this don't need to go fishing for elements that may implement those any more, but can just use on playbin unconditionally.

- multifdsink, tcpclientsink, tcpclientsrc, tcpserversrc the protocol property is removed, use gdppay and gdpdepay.

- XML serialization was removed.

- Probes and pad blocking was merged into new pad probes.

- Position, duration and convert functions no longer use an inout parameter for the destination format.

- Video and audio caps were simplified. audio/x-raw-int and audio/x-raw-float are now all under the audio/x-raw media type. Similarly, video/x-raw-rgb and video/x-raw-yuv are now video/x-raw.

- ffmpegcolorspace was removed and replaced with videoconvert.

- GstMixerInterface / GstTunerInterface were removed without replacement.

- The GstXOverlay interface was renamed to GstVideoOverlay, and now part of the video library in gst-plugins-base, as the interfaces library no longer exists.

  The name of the GstXOverlay "prepare-xwindow-id" message has changed to "prepare-window-handle" (and GstXOverlay has been renamed to GstVideoOverlay). Code that checks for the string directly should be changed to use gst_is_video_overlay_prepare_window_handle_message(message) instead.

- The GstPropertyProbe interface was removed. There is no replacement for it in GStreamer 1.0.x and 1.2.x, but since version 1.4 there is a more featureful replacement for device discovery and feature querying provided by GstDeviceMonitor, GstDevice, and friends. See the "GStreamer Device Discovery and Device Probing" documentation (http://gstreamer.freedesktop.org/data/doc/gstreamer/head/gstreamer/html/gstreamer-device-probing.html).

- gst_uri_handler_get_uri() and the get_uri vfunc now return a copy of the URI string

  gst_uri_handler_set_uri() and the set_uri vfunc now take an additional GError argument so the handler can notify the caller why it didn't accept a particular URI.

  gst_uri_handler_set_uri() now checks if the protocol of the URI passed is one of the protocols advertised by the uri handler, so set_uri vfunc implementations no longer need to check that as well.

- GstTagList is now an opaque mini object instead of being typedefed to a GstStructure. While it was previously okay (and in some cases required because of missing taglist API) to cast a GstTagList to a GstStructure or use gst_structure_* API on taglists, you can no longer do that. Doing so will cause crashes.

  Also, tag lists are refcounted now, and can therefore not be freely modified any longer. Make sure to call gst_tag_list_make_writable (taglist) before adding, removing or changing tags in the taglist.

  GST_TAG_IMAGE, GST_TAG_PREVIEW_IMAGE, GST_TAG_ATTACHMENT: many tags that used to be of type GstBuffer are now of type GstSample (which is basically a struct containing a buffer alongside caps and some other info).

- GstController has now been merged into GstObject. It does not exists as an individual object anymore. In addition core contains a GstControlSource base class and the GstControlBinding. The actual control sources are in the controller library as before. The 2nd big change is that control sources generate a sequence of gdouble values and those are mapped to the property type and value range by GstControlBindings.

The whole gst_controller_* API is gone and now available in simplified form under gst_object_*. ControlSources are now attached via GstControlBinding to properties. There are no GValue arguments used anymore when programming control sources.

Chapter 26. Integration

GStreamer tries to integrate closely with operating systems (such as Linux and UNIX-like operating systems, OS X or Windows) and desktop environments (such as GNOME or KDE). In this chapter, we'll mention some specific techniques to integrate your application with your operating system or desktop environment of choice.

26.1. Linux and UNIX-like operating systems

GStreamer provides a basic set of elements that are useful when integrating with Linux or a UNIX-like operating system.

- For audio input and output, GStreamer provides input and output elements for several audio subsystems. Amongst others, GStreamer includes elements for ALSA (alsasrc, alsasink), OSS (osssrc, osssink) Pulesaudio (pulsesrc, pulsesink) and Sun audio (sunaudiosrc, sunaudiomixer, sunaudiosink).

- For video input, GStreamer contains source elements for Video4linux2 (v4l2src, v4l2element, v4l2sink).

- For video output, GStreamer provides elements for output to X-windows (ximagesink), Xv-windows (xvimagesink; for hardware-accelerated video), direct-framebuffer (dfbimagesink) and openGL image contexts (glsink).

26.2. GNOME desktop

GStreamer has been the media backend of the GNOME (http://www.gnome.org/) desktop since GNOME-2.2 onwards. Nowadays, a whole bunch of GNOME applications make use of GStreamer for media-processing, including (but not limited to) Rhythmbox (http://www.rhythmbox.org/), Videos (https://wiki.gnome.org/Apps/Videos) and Sound Juicer (https://wiki.gnome.org/Apps/SoundJuicer).

Most of these GNOME applications make use of some specific techniques to integrate as closely as possible with the GNOME desktop:

- GNOME applications usually call `gtk_init` () to parse command-line options and initialize GTK. GStreamer applications would normally call `gst_init` () to do the same for GStreamer. This would mean that only one of the two can parse command-line options. To work around this issue, GStreamer can provide a GLib `GOptionGroup` which can be passed to `gnome_program_init` (). The following example requires GTK 2.6 or newer (previous GTK versions do not support command line parsing via GOption yet)

```
#include <gtk/gtk.h>
#include <gst/gst.h>

static gchar **cmd_filenames = NULL;
```

```
static GOptionEntries cmd_options[] = {
  /* here you can add command line options for your application. Check
   * the GOption section in the GLib API reference for a more elaborate
   * example of how to add your own command line options here */

  /* at the end we have a special option that collects all remaining
   * command line arguments (like filenames) for us. If you don't
   * need this, you can safely remove it */
  { G_OPTION_REMAINING, 0, 0, G_OPTION_ARG_FILENAME_ARRAY, &cmd_filenames,
    "Special option that collects any remaining arguments for us" },

  /* mark the end of the options array with a NULL option */
  { NULL, }
};

/* this should usually be defined in your config.h */
#define VERSION "0.0.1"

gint
main (gint argc, gchar **argv)
{
  GOptionContext *context;
  GOptionGroup *gstreamer_group, *gtk_group;
  GError *err = NULL;

  context = g_option_context_new ("gtk-demo-app");

  /* get command line options from GStreamer and add them to the group */
  gstreamer_group = gst_init_get_option_group ();
  g_option_context_add_group (context, gstreamer_group);
  gtk_group = gtk_get_option_group (TRUE);
  g_option_context_add_group (context, gtk_group);

  /* add our own options. If you are using gettext for translation of your
   * strings, use GETTEXT_PACKAGE here instead of NULL */
  g_option_context_add_main_entries (context, cmd_options, NULL);

  /* now parse the commandline options, note that this already
   * calls gtk_init() and gst_init() */
  if (!g_option_context_parse (ctx, &argc, &argv, &err)) {
    g_print ("Error initializing: %s\n", err->message);
    g_clear_error (&err);
    g_option_context_free (ctx);
    exit (1);
  }
  g_option_context_free (ctx);

  /* any filenames we got passed on the command line? parse them! */
  if (cmd_filenames != NULL) {
    guint i, num;

    num = g_strv_length (cmd_filenames);
    for (i = 0; i < num; ++i) {
```

```
        /* do something with the filename ... */
        g_print ("Adding to play queue: %s\n", cmd_filenames[i]);
    }

    g_strfreev (cmd_filenames);
    cmd_filenames = NULL;
  }

[..]

}
```

- GNOME uses Pulseaudio for audio, use the pulsesrc and pulsesink elements to have access to all the features.

- GStreamer provides data input/output elements for use with the GIO VFS system. These elements are called "giosrc" and "giosink". The deprecated GNOME-VFS system is supported too but shouldn't be used for any new applications.

26.3. KDE desktop

GStreamer has been proposed for inclusion in KDE-4.0. Currently, GStreamer is included as an optional component, and it's used by several KDE applications, including AmaroK (http://amarok.kde.org/), KMPlayer (http://www.xs4all.nl/~jjvrieze/kmplayer.html) and Kaffeine (http://kaffeine.sourceforge.net/).

Although not yet as complete as the GNOME integration bits, there are already some KDE integration specifics available. This list will probably grow as GStreamer starts to be used in KDE-4.0:

- AmaroK contains a kiosrc element, which is a source element that integrates with the KDE VFS subsystem KIO.

26.4. OS X

GStreamer provides native video and audio output elements for OS X. It builds using the standard development tools for OS X.

26.5. Windows

Warning

Note: this section is out of date. GStreamer-1.0 has much better support for win32 than previous versions though and should usually compile and work out-of-the-box both using MSYS/MinGW or Microsoft compilers. The GStreamer web site (http://gstreamer.freedesktop.org) and the mailing list archives (http://news.gmane.org/gmane.comp.video.gstreamer.devel) are a good place to check the latest win32-related news.

GStreamer builds using Microsoft Visual C .NET 2003 and using Cygwin.

26.5.1. Building GStreamer under Win32

There are different makefiles that can be used to build GStreamer with the usual Microsoft compiling tools.

The Makefile is meant to be used with the GNU make program and the free version of the Microsoft compiler (http://msdn.microsoft.com/visualc/vctoolkit2003/). You also have to modify your system environment variables to use it from the command-line. You will also need a working Platform SDK for Windows that is available for free from Microsoft.

The projects/makefiles will generate automatically some source files needed to compile GStreamer. That requires that you have installed on your system some GNU tools and that they are available in your system PATH.

The GStreamer project depends on other libraries, namely :

- GLib
- libxml2
- libintl
- libiconv

Work is being done to provide pre-compiled GStreamer-1.0 libraries as a packages for win32. Check the GStreamer web site (http://gstreamer.freedesktop.org) and check our mailing list (http://news.gmane.org/gmane.comp.video.gstreamer.devel) for the latest developments in this respect.

Notes: GNU tools needed that you can find on http://gnuwin32.sourceforge.net/

- GNU flex (tested with 2.5.4)
- GNU bison (tested with 1.35)

and http://www.mingw.org/

- GNU make (tested with 3.80)

the generated files from the -auto makefiles will be available soon separately on the net for convenience (people who don't want to install GNU tools).

26.5.2. Installation on the system

FIXME: This section needs be updated for GStreamer-1.0.

Chapter 27. Licensing advisory

27.1. How to license the applications you build with GStreamer

The licensing of GStreamer is no different from a lot of other libraries out there like GTK+ or glibc: we use the LGPL. What complicates things with regards to GStreamer is its plugin-based design and the heavily patented and proprietary nature of many multimedia codecs. While patents on software are currently only allowed in a small minority of world countries (the US and Australia being the most important of those), the problem is that due to the central place the US hold in the world economy and the computing industry, software patents are hard to ignore wherever you are. Due to this situation, many companies, including major GNU/Linux distributions, get trapped in a situation where they either get bad reviews due to lacking out-of-the-box media playback capabilities (and attempts to educate the reviewers have met with little success so far), or go against their own - and the free software movement's - wish to avoid proprietary software. Due to competitive pressure, most choose to add some support. Doing that through pure free software solutions would have them risk heavy litigation and punishment from patent owners. So when the decision is made to include support for patented codecs, it leaves them the choice of either using special proprietary applications, or try to integrate the support for these codecs through proprietary plugins into the multimedia infrastructure provided by GStreamer. Faced with one of these two evils the GStreamer community of course prefer the second option.

The problem which arises is that most free software and open source applications developed use the GPL as their license. While this is generally a good thing, it creates a dilemma for people who want to put together a distribution. The dilemma they face is that if they include proprietary plugins in GStreamer to support patented formats in a way that is legal for them, they do risk running afoul of the GPL license of the applications. We have gotten some conflicting reports from lawyers on whether this is actually a problem, but the official stance of the FSF is that it is a problem. We view the FSF as an authority on this matter, so we are inclined to follow their interpretation of the GPL license.

So what does this mean for you as an application developer? Well, it means you have to make an active decision on whether you want your application to be used together with proprietary plugins or not. What you decide here will also influence the chances of commercial distributions and Unix vendors shipping your application. The GStreamer community suggest you license your software using a license that will allow proprietary plugins to be bundled with GStreamer and your applications, in order to make sure that as many vendors as possible go with GStreamer instead of less free solutions. This in turn we hope and think will let GStreamer be a vehicle for wider use of free formats like the Xiph.org formats.

If you do decide that you want to allow for non-free plugins to be used with your application you have a variety of choices. One of the simplest is using licenses like LGPL, MPL or BSD for your application instead of the GPL. Or you can add an exception clause to your GPL license stating that you except GStreamer plugins from the obligations of the GPL.

A good example of such a GPL exception clause would be, using the Totem video player project as an example: The authors of the Totem video player project hereby grants permission for non-GPL-compatible GStreamer plugins to be used and distributed together with GStreamer and Totem. This permission goes above and beyond the permissions granted by the GPL license Totem is covered by.

Our suggestion among these choices is to use the LGPL license, as it is what resembles the GPL most and it makes it a good licensing fit with the major GNU/Linux desktop projects like GNOME and KDE. It also allows you to share code more openly with projects that have compatible licenses. Obviously, pure GPL code without the above-mentioned clause is not usable in your application as such. By choosing the LGPL, there is no need for an exception clause and thus code can be shared more freely.

I have above outlined the practical reasons for why the GStreamer community suggests you allow non-free plugins to be used with your applications. We feel that in the multimedia arena, the free software community is still not strong enough to set the agenda and that blocking non-free plugins to be used in our infrastructure hurts us more than it hurts the patent owners and their ilk.

This view is not shared by everyone. The Free Software Foundation urges you to use an unmodified GPL for your applications, so as to push back against the temptation to use non-free plug-ins. They say that since not everyone else has the strength to reject them because they are unethical, they ask your help to give them a legal reason to do so.

This advisory is part of a bigger advisory with a FAQ which you can find on the GStreamer website (http://gstreamer.freedesktop.org/documentation/licensing.html)

Chapter 28. Quotes from the Developers

As well as being a cool piece of software, GStreamer is a lively project, with developers from around the globe very actively contributing. We often hang out on the #gstreamer IRC channel on irc.freenode.net: the following are a selection of amusing[1] quotes from our conversations.

6 Mar 2006

> When I opened my eyes I was in a court room. There were masters McIlroy and Thompson sitting in the jury and master Kernighan too. There were the GStreamer developers standing in the defendant's place, accused of violating several laws of Unix philosophy and customer lock-down via running on a proprietary pipeline, different from that of the Unix systems. I heard Eric Raymond whispering "got to add this case to my book.
>
> *behdad's blog*

22 May 2007

> <*__tim*> Uraeus: amusing, isn't it?
>
> <*Uraeus*> __tim: I wrote that :)
>
> <*__tim*> Uraeus: of course you did; your refusal to surrender to the oppressive regime of the third-person-singular-rule is so unique in its persistence that it's hard to miss :)

12 Sep 2005

> <*wingo*> we just need to get rid of that mmap stuff
>
> <*wingo*> i think gnomevfssrc is faster for files even
>
> <*BBB*> wingo, no
>
> <*BBB*> and no
>
> <*wingo*> good points ronald

23 Jun 2005

> * *wingo* back
>
> * *thomasvs* back

--- You are now known as everybody

* *everybody* back back

<*everybody*> now break it down

--- You are now known as thomasvs

* *bilboed* back

--- bilboed is now known as john-sebastian

* *john-sebastian* bach

--- john-sebastian is now known as bilboed

--- You are now known as scratch_my

* *scratch_my* back

--- bilboed is now known as Illbe

--- You are now known as thomasvs

* *Illbe* back

--- Illbe is now known as bilboed

20 Apr 2005

thomas: jrb, somehow his screenshotsrc grabs whatever X is showing and makes it available as a stream of frames

jrb: thomas: so, is the point that the screenshooter takes a video? but won't the dialog be in the video? oh, nevermind. I'll just send mail...

thomas: jrb, well, it would shoot first and ask questions later

2 Nov 2004

    zaheerm: wtay: unfair u fixed the bug i was using as a feature!

14 Oct 2004

    * *zaheerm* wonders how he can break gstreamer today :)

    ensonic: zaheerm, spider is always a good starting point

14 Jun 2004

    teuf: ok, things work much better when I don't write incredibly stupid and buggy code

    thaytan: I find that too

23 Nov 2003

    Uraeus: ah yes, the sleeping part, my mind is not multitasking so I was still thinking about exercise

    dolphy: Uraeus: your mind is multitasking

    dolphy: Uraeus: you just miss low latency patches

14 Sep 2002

    --- *wingo-party* is now known as *wingo*

    * *wingo* holds head

4 Jun 2001

    taaz: you witchdoctors and your voodoo mpeg2 black magic...

    omega_: um. I count three, no four different cults there <g>

    ajmitch: hehe

    omega_: witchdoctors, voodoo, black magic,

    omega_: and mpeg

16 Feb 2001

> *wtay:* I shipped a few commerical products to >40000 people now but GStreamer is way more
> exciting...

16 Feb 2001

> * *tool-man* is a gstreamer groupie

14 Jan 2001

> *Omega:* did you run ldconfig? maybe it talks to init?

> *wtay:* not sure, don't think so... I did run gstreamer-register though :-)

> *Omega:* ah, that did it then ;-)

> *wtay:* right

> *Omega:* probably not, but in case GStreamer starts turning into an OS, someone please let me know?

9 Jan 2001

> *wtay:* me tar, you rpm?

> *wtay:* hehe, forgot "zan"

> *Omega:* ?

> *wtay:* me tar"zan", you ...

7 Jan 2001

> *Omega:* that means probably building an agreggating, cache-massaging queue to shove N buffers
> across all at once, forcing cache transfer.

> *wtay:* never done that before...

> *Omega:* nope, but it's easy to do in gstreamer <g>

> *wtay:* sure, I need to rewrite cp with gstreamer too, someday :-)

7 Jan 2001

> *wtay:* GStreamer; always at least one developer is awake...

5/6 Jan 2001

> *wtay:* we need to cut down the time to create an mp3 player down to seconds...

> *richardb:* :)

> *Omega:* I'm wanting to something more interesting soon, I did the "draw an mp3 player in 15sec" back in October '99.

> *wtay:* by the time Omega gets his hands on the editor, you'll see a complete audio mixer in the editor :-)

> *richardb:* Well, it clearly has the potential...

> *Omega:* Working on it... ;-)

28 Dec 2000

> *MPAA:* We will sue you now, you have violated our IP rights!

> *wtay:* hehehe

> *MPAA:* How dare you laugh at us? We have lawyers! We have Congressmen! We have *LARS*!

> *wtay:* I'm so sorry your honor

> *MPAA:* Hrumph.

> * *wtay* bows before thy

Notes

1. No guarantee of sense of humour compatibility is given.